Understanding your emotions...

ANGER

Learning about the positive and Negative aspect of the most misunderstood emotion

By

Caroline J. Collins

Copyright © by Caroline J. Collins 2023. All rights reserved.

Before this document is duplicated or reproduced in any manner, the publisher's consent must be gained. Therefore, the contents within can neither be stored electronically, transferred, nor kept in a database. Neither in Part nor full can the document be copied, scanned, faxed, or retained without approval from the publisher or creator.

Table of content

Understanding your emotions…ANGER

INTRODUCTION

Chapter 1: Understanding Anger
What causes people to become angry?
Physiology of Anger
Purpose and Benefits of anger
Anger and other emotions

Chapter 2: The Positive Aspects of Anger
Positive effects of anger
Problems of suppressing or ignoring Anger
How to use Anger as a Motivator
Using anger to effect positive change

Chapter 3: The Negative aspects of anger
Effects of Being Angry All the Time on Your Body
Negative Effects of Anger

Chapter 4: Types of Anger
Passive Aggression
Assertive Anger
Other forms of anger

Chapter 5: Anger Management
Anger management techniques
Importance of anger management exercises

Conclusion

INTRODUCTION

Anger is a fundamental human emotion that is defined by the emotions of irritation, aggravation, anger, or wrath. It is a normal reaction to perceived danger or injustice, and it may be triggered by a broad variety of events, including interpersonal disputes, physical discomfort, or perceived unfairness.

Anger is a complicated emotion that may be expressed in a number of ways, ranging from slight annoyance to severe anger. It may also be conveyed verbally or physically, and it can have both positive and negative repercussions.

On one side, anger may also serve as a beneficial weapon for encouraging change and confronting injustice. It energizes individuals to take action against social and political injustice or may assist someone in defending themselves against personal and professional maltreatment.

On the other Anger may also have negative implications when displayed in the wrong way; anger can lead to aggressiveness, violence, and other damaging actions. It may also destroy personal relationships, weaken professional reputations, and lead to legal implications.

Anger is a tool that has both a bad and a beneficial side depending on how you express and handle it.

Learning how to handle anger is a highly unique talent that may assist people in traversing challenging circumstances and accomplishing their objectives.

Chapter 1

Understanding Anger

Anger is a natural and largely automatic reaction to pain of some kind. Anger can arise when someone does not feel well, is rejected, is threatened, or has suffered a loss. The type of pain does not matter; what matters is that the pain is unpleasant. Because Anger is never experienced in isolation but is always preceded by pain feelings, it is frequently referred to as a secondhand or substitute emotion.

Anger as a substitute

Anger can also function as a substitute emotion. This means that people will occasionally make themselves angry in order to avoid feeling pain. People convert their suffering into anger because it feels better to be angry than to be in pain. This transformation of grief into anger can occur intentionally or unconsciously.

Being Angry rather than simply in pain provides a number of advantages, the most important of which is diversion. People who are in agony frequently think about their discomfort. However, angry people consider harming those who have caused them distress. An attention shift from self-focus to other-focus is involved in the transformation of pain into anger .

Thus, anger momentarily shelters people from having to confront and deal with their terrible genuine sentiments; instead, you worry about getting back at the people you're upset with. Making yourself furious can help you hide the fact that you are afraid of a situation or feel vulnerable.

In addition to acting as an effective mask for feelings of vulnerability, becoming furious gives a sense of righteousness, authority, and moral superiority that does not exist when someone is simply in pain. When you are angry, you are angry for a reason. "Those who have harmed me are wrong, and they should be punished," is a familiar refrain. It is quite rare for someone to become enraged at someone who they do not believe has injured them significantly.

Anger is a universal human emotion that everyone feels. Anger is typically experienced as an unpleasant feeling that happens when we believe we have been damaged, mistreated, opposed in our long-held beliefs, or when we confront hurdles that prevent us from achieving personal goals. The feeling of anger varies greatly; how frequently anger arises, how powerfully it is felt, and how long it lasts differ for each individual. People also differ in terms of how readily they become angry and how comfortable they are with feeling angry.

Some people are usually angry, while others are rarely angry. Some people are acutely aware of their anger, whereas others fail to notice it when it arises.

The average adult experiences anger about once per day and irritation or resentment about three times per day, according to some experts. Other anger management experts believe that being furious fifteen times per day is a more realistic average. Regardless of how frequently we experience it, anger is a prevalent and unavoidable emotion.

Anger has the potential to be both useful and destructive. Anger or displeasure has little negative health or interpersonal implications when it is appropriately managed. Anger is a notice to you that something isn't right in your environment. It grabs your attention and pushes you to take action to fix the error. However, how you handle the anger signal has far-reaching implications for your general health and well-being. When you express your anger, it causes others to become defensive and furious as well. Blood pressure rises, and stress chemicals are released. Violence may erupt. You can earn a reputation as a hazardous "loose cannon" who no one wants to be around.

Anger that is out of control alienates friends, coworkers, and family members. It also has a clear link to health issues and early mortality. Hostile, violent Anger not only raises your risk of dying young, but it also increases your risk of social isolation, which is a key risk factor for serious disease and mortality.

These are only two of the numerous reasons why learning to manage one's anger is a good thing.

Anger can be exhibited in a variety of ways; different types of anger have varied effects on people and can show in a variety of actions and signals of anger. Anger manifests itself in both verbal and nonverbal ways.

It can be obvious that someone is angry based on what they say, how they say it, or the tone of their voice. Anger can also be exhibited by body language and other nonverbal signs, such as trying to appear physically bigger (and so more scary), glaring, frowning, and fist clenching. Some people are quite excellent at suppressing their anger, making it impossible to detect any outward manifestations. It is, nevertheless, unusual for a physical attack to occur without 'warning' indications initially showing.

What causes people to become angry?

Anger can be utilized instinctively to assist protect territory or family members, obtain or protect mating privileges, protect against loss of food or other goods, or respond to other perceived dangers.

Other reasons can be quite varied, sometimes rational, sometimes irrational.

Irrational anger may indicate a problem with anger management or even accepting that you are upset.

The following are some typical irritants:
- sadness and/or grief following the death of a friend, family member, or other loved one.
- Discourteousness, poor relational abilities, or potentially unfortunate assistance. Tiredness, as tired people may have a shorter temper and be more irritable.
- Hunger.
- Injustice: for instance, being told you or a loved one has a serious illness, being bullied, humiliated, or embarrassed, or being the victim of infidelity.
- Sexual disappointment.
- problems with money and the stress that comes with having debt.
- Some kinds of stress, deadlines that aren't realistic, and things we can't control right now, like getting stuck in traffic.
- Having a furious reaction to ingesting drink or drugs or withdrawing from them
- Committing a crime against oneself or a loved one: burglary, ruthlessness, sexual offenses, yet additionally more minor things, for example, a sensation of being dealt with improperly.
- Angry feelings can result from physical or mental illness, pain, or living with a serious illness.

Physiology of Anger

Like different feelings, anger is knowledgeable about our bodies as well as our psyches. In point of fact, when we become enraged, a complex series of physiological (body) events take place.

The amygdala, two structures in our brains shaped like almonds is where emotions start. The amygdala is the part of the brain that identifies threats to our well-being and sends out an alarm when threats are identified, prompting us to take measures to safeguard ourselves. The amygdala is so good at telling us about dangers that it gets us to act before the cortex, which is in charge of thinking and making decisions, can see if our actions are reasonable. To put it another way, our brains are wired in a way that makes us want to do something before we can really think about what will happen. This isn't a reason for acting seriously; individuals can and do control their forceful motivations, and you can too with some training. All things considered, it implies that figuring out how to oversee anger appropriately is an expertise that must be mastered rather than something we are conceived knowing how to do instinctively.

The muscles in your body tighten when you get angry. Inside your mind, synapse synthetic substances known as catecholamines are delivered, making you experience an eruption of energy that lasts as long as a few minutes.

The common angry desire to take immediate protective measures is caused by this burst of energy.

Your heart rate accelerates, your blood pressure rises, and your breathing rate accelerates simultaneously. As your limbs and legs receive more blood in preparation for physical activity, your face may flush. Your consideration limits and becomes locked onto the objective of your annoyance. Soon, you won't be able to focus on anything else. Additional brain neurotransmitters and hormones, including adrenaline and noradrenaline, are released in rapid succession, resulting in a persistent state of arousal. Now is the time to fight.

Despite the fact that it is feasible for your feelings to go crazy, the prefrontal cortex of your mind, which is found simply behind your brow, can keep your feelings in check. The prefrontal cortex handles judgment, while the amygdala controls emotion. Your emotions can be turned off by the left prefrontal cortex. To keep things under control, it acts as an executive. Learning strategies to assist your prefrontal cortex in gaining control over your amygdala is an essential step in gaining control over your anger. Relaxation techniques, which lower your arousal and lower the activity of your amygdala, and cognitive control techniques, which help you practice using your judgment to override your emotional reactions, are two of the many ways to achieve this.

Anger has a breeze down the stage as well as a physiological ease with which our assets are prepared for a battle.

When the object of our anger is no longer accessible or poses an immediate threat, we begin to relax into a state of rest. However, it is difficult to unwind after being angry. The adrenaline-caused excitement that happens during anger endures seemingly forever (numerous hours, some of the time days) and brings down our annoyance edge, making it simpler for us to lash out once more some other time on. We do calm down, but it takes a very long time for us to go back to sleeping. We are more likely to become extremely irate in response to minor irritations that normally would not bother us during this slow cooling-off period.

The same persistent arousal that keeps us poised for additional anger can also make it harder for us to remember the nuances of our anger . Arousal is necessary for effective memory. Any student knows that it's hard to learn new information when you're tired. The brain learns and improves memory, concentration, and performance at moderate levels of arousal. However, there is an optimal level of arousal that is good for memory, and when arousal goes above that level, it makes it harder to make new memories. Concentration is significantly impaired when you experience high levels of arousal, like when you are angry. It's hard to remember the specifics of really heated arguments because of this.

Purpose and Benefits of anger

The goal of anger is to quickly encourage decision-making, reduce options, or avoid further deviating from the ideal situation.

The mind perceives a threat when things diverge from the ideal as a result of something or someone (whoever they attribute the blame to). In response, it develops negative emotions. An emotion is elicited (anxiety, fear, anger, dread, irritation) depending on the speed of the distraction, the anticipated outcome, and the potential for change.

Most of the time, people get angry and irritated when they feel like they could do something about a bad situation but are forced to hold back, either by themselves or by others. It builds up to a point where it snaps, and then the anger drives the action to be carried out quickly.

Taking the offending agent, person, or object out of the way (by hindering, insulting, hurting, killing, or destroying) is typically the action that prevents further detracting from the ideal situation. Some people view this as an option that limits or reduces motivation.

It is a useful emotion in uncivilized times for making quick decisions that could save a life or end it. In today's world, it can still be useful in some situations, but it usually has a negative effect on relationships when anger is expressed uncontrollably.

However, anger is useful. The adrenaline and stress hormones can be channeled into productivity, functioning like eustress, in addition to the fact that you need to experience unpleasant emotions like anger to be truly satisfied.

Anger has the following advantages:

Boosts your enthusiasm: The survival chemicals of anger increase your inspiration to travel through a circumstance. On the off chance that your manager imposes a cutoff time you view as outlandish, which drives you mad, you may be roused to attempt to meet it to demonstrate you're fit for taking on additional significant undertakings.

Aids in setting boundaries: You might learn to establish new boundaries with other people as you work through conflict so that you don't get angry again. Knowing what's best for your body and mind will help you organize a life that works for you, even if that means avoiding a certain coworker or finding a commute that doesn't involve as much traffic.

Focuses on conflict resolution: Either yelling at a loved one or holding in your emotions does nothing to relieve tension or stress.

However, you will be better able to resolve conflict in both personal and professional relationships if you learn to express your anger in a healthy and respectful manner. This helps you learn more about other people and improves your ability to resolve conflicts, whether at work or at home.

Fulfills your requirements: anger cautions you that something doesn't cause you to feel content and that it needs to change. It could demonstrate to you that you place a high value on honesty in your relationships, and as time goes on, you will work to satisfy that need because it is important to you.

Improves self-esteem: Even if you don't think of yourself as an angry person, you might start using techniques for controlling your temper. These methods might help you get to know yourself better and show you how much control you have over your life

Makes one more aware of oneself: Why are you angry? What initially causes these feelings of anger in you? When you start to think about these things, you'll become more aware of yourself. In addition, you will gain a deeper understanding of who you are and what you want out of life, such as what kind of career would be most meaningful to you.

The proper method to express anger

Anger can only serve you if you know how to control it. You may be furious at work but don't know how to express yourself properly and appropriately to your supervisor, resulting in stress and poor working relationships. And if your partner annoys you and your outbursts of anger are unhealthy, your relationship may suffer.

As a result, understanding appropriate ways to express anger will help you gain control of your emotions and situation. Here are five suggestions to help you express your anger more effectively with others:

1. Consider the power of your words.

In the heat of the moment, you may feel compelled to utter every thought that comes to mind. Nonetheless, words have great power and have the capacity to harm others around you. Being attentive to your word choice will assist you in avoiding hurtful statements and maintaining your professional and personal relationships.

2. Generate solutions

It's fine to be angry, but what will you do about it? Consider thinking of solutions to make good change while you're expressing your feelings. Consider how you might avoid feeling upset in the future.

To better understand others, you could practice being more patient or listening to their points of view.

3. Be truthful.
Now is not the time to sugarcoat your feelings. Stand up for yourself and be open about how you feel. Your loved ones and friends may be unaware of what bothers you because you are never honest about it. But being truthful does not imply the absence of a filter. Select your words carefully, and keep in mind that they have power.

4. Exercise accountability.
Your anger is entirely your own. Being accountable means accepting responsibility for your feelings and working through them rather than blaming someone or anything else.
Consider utilizing "I" phrases instead of "you" when discussing what causes you to have an emotional response like this. To keep your thoughts and feelings in the forefront, instead of saying, "You made me feel this way," say, "I felt this way."

5. Be mindful of your tone.
There's no getting around it: Your emotional reaction will be emotional. Your anger may reflect these emotions, which may be accompanied by feelings of betrayal, bitterness, or frustration.

Monitoring your tone entails being aware of how loudly you talk and how respectfully your words are delivered. Instead of shouting, which may encourage more aggressive behavior, try slowing down your speech. It will assist you in regaining control.

Anger and other emotions

Wrath and Anger
Wrath and anger are two distinct concepts with distinct meanings, despite the fact that they both allude to a person's discontent or anger. Wrath is one of the seven deadly sins, according to Christianity. This demonstrates that, in contrast to anger, wrath is a considerably more powerful emotion. We have a discontent called anger. Yet, anger is more than just disapproval; it is anger with malicious intent. For example, a person may grow upset, shout, and have unpleasant thoughts toward another person, yet he eventually overcomes these feelings. It is not so straightforward in wrath. His wrath grows stronger with the passage of time.

Wrath is the ultimate version of anger, whereas anger is a strong sense of annoyance, displeasure, or animosity.

Anger is a universal emotion shared by all living things. When anger progresses from feeling to action, it becomes wrath.

As a result, anger is an extreme form of anger that includes violence or violent deeds. Wrath, on the other hand, is not healthy or socially acceptable.

Anger is a powerful, typically hostile emotion that you experience when you believe someone has treated you unfairly, cruelly, or in an undesirable manner. It is a universal emotional reaction shared by all living things. Anger is typically a reaction to emotional discomfort; it is a reaction to a threat, pain, criticism, or perceived provocation. It can also be a secondary reaction to feelings of loneliness, sadness, or fear.

Anger affects us differently depending on how we express it, how intense it is, how long it lasts, and so on. Some people are usually angry, while others are rarely angry. Anger can be expressed verbally as well as nonverbally. External expressions of anger include facial expressions, body language, physiological responses, and aggressive behaviors.

Anger is seen by psychologists as a normal and natural reaction, and it can be either constructive or destructive, implying that it can have both positive and negative consequences. Anger is a signal to you that something in your surroundings isn't right, and it inspires you to take action to repair that wrong. The negative consequences of anger are related to how you manage or regulate your anger. Persistent and intense anger can have a number of negative health consequences, including stress and an increase in blood pressure.

Furthermore, uncontrollable anger can turn you violent and destructive, separating you from family, friends, and coworkers and leading to social isolation.

As a result, regulating your anger is critical to living a healthy existence.

What exactly is wrath?

Wrath is a severe sort of anger. To put it another way, it entails violence or violent deeds. It is characterized by extreme aggression, anger, antagonism, hatred, and vengeance. As a consequence of this, wrath is anger that has been transformed into an extreme, uncontrollable, violent emotion that leads to hostile and vengeful actions.

Hatred usually drives a person to engage in damaging behavior toward another individual. Furthermore, anger might be the result of long-repressed anger, a reaction to a significant injustice, or even an inability to manage one's anger. Anger also blurs one's judgment and renders people senseless, resulting in widespread devastation.

Difference between wrath and anger

• Anger is a powerful sense of annoyance that everyone feels when they are wounded or challenged. It is quite normal to be angry.

• Wrath is a severe sort of anger that is both destructive and spiteful. This can lead to severely damaging conduct toward others and even toward oneself.

- Wrath , unlike anger, is one of the seven deadly sins.
- Wrath is unnatural, but anger is natural.
- When an individual is angry, he is aware of what is right and wrong, but when he is enraged, he loses his sense of morality as he is overpowered by hatred.
- Anger is also a natural human emotion; thus, it is allowed, whereas wrath is not.
- Anger is not always destructive or violent; it can also be beneficial. Wrath, on the other hand, inevitably leads to violent deeds, resulting in immense destruction.

Anger and rage
Rage and Anger are closely related, and most individuals do not see a clear distinction between the two. Anger and rage are both emotional outbursts.

Anger is a feeling or emotion that a person has when they are outraged or wronged. Rage can be defined as an action taken in response to a person's anger. Rage is a condition in which a person is unable to control their anger .

Anger is an emotion that everyone experiences. It is simply a sensation, similar to happiness or sorrow.

Rage, then again, is an outrageous type of anger.

Anger is a fleeting feeling that lasts only a few moments or a day at most. If this emotion lasts for an extended period of time, it is called rage . There is no blood shed in anger , yet rage may result in bloodshed.

It can also be seen that anger is regarded as healthy, whereas rage is regarded as unhealthy.

This indicates that a furious individual will have the ability to manage their emotions. Nonetheless, a person experiencing rage has little control over their emotions, which can be destructive at times.

Some argue that rage has an element of anger, but anger lacks the sting of rage. Rage, unlike anger, is a complex blend of dread, desperation, anger, and panic.

It is also possible that people who are enraged forget what they say and do. An angry individual, on the other hand, is aware of what he does and says. Rage, unlike anger, is characterized by a complete blackout of ideas.

• Anger is a feeling or emotion that a person has when they are outraged or wronged.

• Rage can be defined as an action taken in response to a person's anger

• Rage is an extreme form of anger.

• There is no bloodshed in anger , but rage may result in bloodshed.

• Rage is considered unhealthy, whereas anger is considered healthy.

• An angry person has the ability to manage their emotions. Nevertheless, a person in rage lacks emotional control and can be destructive at times.

• Rage, unlike anger, is characterized by a complete blackout of ideas.

Being Mad and Anger

Everyone has been there. We've all felt that red-hot anger well up inside of us, spurred by something minor or major. "I'm so mad!" We might have shouted seemingly out of the blue. But are we truly mad? Or are we just angry? Is there a distinction?

What Does the Phrase "*Mad*" Mean?
It's an informal word to say someone is "mad" in the context of rage or anger. Being "mad" refers to being in a state of high emotional arousal as a result of a perceived provocation. The adjective "mad" used to describe someone angry can be used to emphasize the anger or express the severity of the anger .

Informally, mad refers to the state of being furious or agitated in an inappropriate or impolite manner. It can be used as an adjective to describe someone who is angry or agitated or as a noun to define the emotion itself. Raised voices, clenched fists, and other angry body language are frequently associated with informal madness.

Madness, as slang says, may be an extremely strong feeling that can occasionally lead to terrible conduct. When someone is mad, it's critical to figure out what's causing it. Something may have disturbed the individual, or there may be an underlying issue that has to be addressed.

Being angry can be tough to handle, but the following steps can help:
• Maintain your cool and avoid escalating the situation.
 •It may also be beneficial to discuss your concerns with someone, whether a friend or a professional.
• Try to find healthy ways to vent your anger, such as via exercise or meditation.

When one is "mad" in the meaning of insane or crazy, however, this is a formal phrase. Although the adjective "crazy" has mostly supplanted "mad" as the primary descriptor for mental illness, both are still used. Being "crazy" or "mad" means losing contact with reality and being unable to think or act logically. In general, madness is characterized as a state in which a person's ideas, feelings, or behaviors are considerably impaired or aberrant.

Individuals who are considered mad may experience hallucinations, delusions, paranoia, disorganized thinking, and emotional instability. The intensity of these symptoms varies from person to person, with some experiencing just minor symptoms and others experiencing significant impairment.

There is no single origin of madness; the illness might be caused by heredity, biological changes, environmental circumstances, or psychological factors.

Most mental diseases also have no one cure, and treatment usually consists of a combination of medicine and counseling.
The primary distinction between these two uses of "mad" is their formality. Informal usage is more common and less formal, whereas formal usage is less common and more formal. Both can be used to describe someone who is angry or deranged, but they have different meanings.

What Does the Word "*Anger*" Mean?
Anger is a common and typical emotion that everyone feels at times. It can be useful in a variety of situations, such as encouraging you to act or preserving your rights. But if not conveyed properly, anger can be devastating.
Anger is frequently defined as a state of frustration, or displeasure. Physical feelings such as a racing heart, clenched hands, or a knot in the stomach may accompany it. Anger is typically directed at someone or something, such as being upset with your partner for forgetting to take out the garbage or the government for raising taxes. When someone is upset, they may feel compelled to act in order to release the energy that has accumulated within them.
When one is angry, it is critical to vent one's sentiments in a healthy manner. This entails communicating properly and quietly without yelling or calling someone names. It is equally critical to listen to the other person and attempt to comprehend their point of view.

There are various ways to deal with managing anger. Some people like to express their anger in a healthy way, while others prefer to keep it bottled up. When people choose to vent their anger in a healthy way, they can help release the energy that has been building up inside of them.

When someone decides to bottle their anger, though, it can have negative implications such as tension and anxiety. If you are unable to settle the issue on your own, it may be beneficial to speak with a therapist or counselor who can help you control your anger in a healthy way.

Difference Between Mad and Angry

Anger is an immediate, visceral reaction to a stimulus that is often fleeting. It is an emotional reaction to a circumstance that is typically directed outward (toward the person or thing that caused the anger). Madness, on the other hand, is a longer, more protracted emotional response that may or may not be directed towards a single person or thing. Alternatively, it could be sentiments of general irritation, powerlessness, or even wrath.

The ability to manage one's emotions is a key distinction between being furious and being mad. When people are upset, they usually believe they have some control over their responses and may behave accordingly.

When someone is angry, they frequently believe that their emotions are out of control and that there is nothing they can do to keep them from exploding. This lack of control can be extremely frustrating, leading to even more rage or dissatisfaction

Another distinction between anger and mad is the endurance of the emotion. As previously said, anger is a fleeting feeling; however, being mad can continue for days or weeks after an event has occurred.

This disparity in duration frequently indicates that furious people dwell on the incident for a longer period of time than mad people. This ruminating can result in even worse feelings of irritation or rage. Here are some more distinctions between the two.

Angry cannot be used to describe someone who is eccentric or playful, although mad can.

When someone is angry, they are often full of energy and may appear malicious. Even though they are angry, they may chuckle or smile. When someone is upset, they are usually tense and may have a scowl on their face. They're not going to smile or laugh.

Because mad is more general than angry, it might describe someone who is eccentric or playful. Anger is typically focused on a single person or thing, whereas madness can be aimed at anyone or anything.

Angry statements are frequently accusatory, although mad statements are not always accusatory.

Consider the following scenario: Someone steps on your foot. You might say "Ouch!" or "Look where you're going!" in response to the pain.

The first comment is mad since it is simply a reaction to the incident. The second statement is an angry one since it accuses the other person of wrongdoing.

Frustration or hurt may trigger angry words. We may feel wronged in some way and lash out at the person we believe has wronged us. This can harm our relationships because it makes the other person feel unsafe and insecure around us. In contrast, wild statements aren't necessarily prompted by being mad. These could simply be expressions of how we are feeling at the time.

Because they are motivated by negative emotions, angry words are often more harmful. When we are furious, we are unable to think properly, and our reactions can be harmful to ourselves and others. Angry remarks are simply reactions to what is happening at the time, without the emotional baggage that rage brings.

Madness is usually a reaction to a situation, whereas anger can sometimes be preemptive or retaliatory.

Anger is frequently a reaction to an unjust or inappropriate circumstance. It can be preemptive, like when someone anticipates an attack or insult. When someone reacts to an insult with an insult of their own, it can be considered retaliatory.

Adrenaline and other hormones fuel anger, which frequently leads to impulsive or dangerous conduct.

Crazy, on the other hand, is a deliberate reaction. It is frequently caused by irritation, disappointment, or grief. While anger can sometimes result in positive change, it also frequently results in passivity or resignation. Being mad is sometimes accompanied by feelings of powerlessness or hopelessness.

Anger and anxiety

Anxiety and anger have a lot in common.

By releasing powerful hormones into your circulation, both emotions induce physical discomfort. Both can be caused by commonplace events. And your mental patterns can either improve or degrade both.

Here's what we know about the relationship between anger and anxiety:

A feature of the human condition

Everyone becomes angry. Everyone experiences anxiety from time to time.

In truth, there are moments when fear is justified and anger is a legitimate reaction—one that can result in significant improvements.

Anxiety and anger may appear to be the new normal during times of heightened stress and tension, when issues in your personal life are exacerbated by events in the larger world.

Identical physiological signs

When you are furious or anxious, your body produces hormones such as cortisol and adrenaline that prepare you to fight or run.

You are likely to encounter the following symptoms when you are nervous or angry:

High heart rate

Tightness in the chest

Muscles that are tightened or tight

Heat triggers gastrointestinal symptoms such as diarrhea and tension headaches.

Under typical conditions, these symptoms will fade soon. But if you have long-term troubles with anger or anxiety, the repeated release of these hormones may cause health concerns.

The same psychological foundations

Anxiety and anger have been linked by psychologists to a loss of control.

In other words, when faced with a stressor that you believe you are unprepared to handle, you may become apprehensive.

Anxiety can rapidly turn to anger if you feel even more threatened.

In both cases, external stimulation undermines your sense of safety and control over your surroundings.

Anger could simply be a more chemically powered form of anxiety.

Some psychologists believe that anger is at the basis of anxiety; people who haven't learned how to vent their anger constructively may have protracted periods of anxiety.

Impact on health

If your anger and anxiety feel out of control, or if others tell you that the way you handle your anger and anxiety is causing difficulties, it may be time to get help.

Anger and anxiety can be detrimental to your mental and physical health.

Anger, for example, has been found by researchers to be higher in anxiety and depressive illnesses.

Too much worry and anger can result in: lung cancer issues, such as exacerbated asthma headaches

Cardiovascular disease

Fatigue

Insomnia

The relationship between anger and the fight-or-flight reaction

Anger is the physiological response of the body to a perceived threat to you, your loved ones, your possessions, your self-image, your emotional safety, or another aspect of your identity. The "fight or flight" reaction trains your body to fight or flee in response to a perceived threat to your survival. It's a sign that something is wrong.

This response, which was first documented in the 1920s by Harvard scientist Walter Cannon, is hard-wired into your brain and symbolizes genetic wisdom designed to protect you from bodily harm. This response relates to the hypothalamus, a region of the brain that, when triggered, triggers a series of nerve cell firings and chemical releases that prepare your body for running or fighting.

When the "fight or flight" reaction is triggered, hormones like adrenaline, noradrenaline, and cortisol are released into the bloodstream, causing a cascade of dramatic changes. They are referred to as mind and body indicators. Common mental and physical symptoms include:

• Rapid breathing and rapid heartbeat
• An upset stomach or a tight stomach
• Muscle tenseness
• Migraine
• Difficulty concentrating
• A sense of helplessness and impotence

The "fight or flight" system, by definition, bypasses the rational mind, where more well-thought-out beliefs exist, and places you in an "attack" state. Fear distorts your thinking and becomes the lens through which you view the world.

"Fight or flight" is a reaction that is warranted in life-threatening situations, but most anger situations are not. They are concerned with circumstances that are based on values and judgments rather than risks. When you acknowledge that you are not in danger, you have the option of responding or not responding.

You can learn to respond rather than react if you notice the cognitive and body signals of "fight or flight" activation.

The Medol Model is used in all Anger Alternatives programs to build heightened awareness and mental acuity to:
• Alter your emotional surroundings
• Foster emotional literacy and
• Use communication techniques that foster respectful relationships.

Anger is something that everyone feels, and it can be beneficial. When you hear the message of anger, it can push you to defend yourself. Embracing anger can lead to beneficial improvements in your life and relationships. An innate physiological response to a stressful or frightening situation is the fight-or-flight experience. When a threat is perceived, the sympathetic nervous system is activated, triggering an acute stress response that prepares the body to fight or flee. These responses are evolutionary adaptations that boost the likelihood of surviving in dangerous conditions.

Excessive, severe, or inappropriate activation of the fight-or-flight response has been linked to a variety of clinical problems, including the majority of anxiety disorders. An important part of treating anxiety is learning more about the fight-or-flight response's purpose and function. The physical effects of the fight-or-flight reaction are described in this client information sheet.

During the fight-or-flight response, the sympathetic nervous system is activated. The fight or flight response can set off a chain reaction that can result in the following physical effects:

Heart rate increase; dilation of coronary blood vessels; increased blood flow Improved oxygen and energy availability to the heart.

Circulation: dilation of blood vessels serving muscles; constriction of blood vessels serving digestion; increased oxygen availability to skeletal muscles; blood directed to skeletal muscles and the brain.

Lungs: bronchial dilation; increased breathing rate; increased oxygen availability in blood

Increased glycogen to glucose conversion in the liver; increased glucose availability in skeletal muscle and brain cells

Skin: As blood flow drops, the skin becomes pale or flushed, with increased blood flow to muscles and away from non-essential regions of the body like the periphery.

Eyes: Dilation of the pupils lets in more light, improving visual acuity to monitor close surroundings.

In addition to physiological reactions, the fight-or-flight response has a psychological component. A speeding of thought and an attentional concentration on conspicuous objectives such as the source of the threat and potential escape routes are examples of automatic reactions. Secondary psychological responses can involve evaluations of the significance of bodily events. Patients with panic disorder, for example, frequently misunderstand fight or flight responses as indicators of impending disaster

Why is the fight-or-flight response necessary?
The physiological reactions linked with fight or flight can be important in surviving truly dangerous situations. Nonetheless, many patients suffering from anxiety disorders or other illnesses may have overactive threat systems that are insufficiently counterbalanced by parasympathetic nervous system activity.
Many patients who suffer from anxiety can benefit from a better understanding of the fight-or-flight response in practice. Patients suffering from panic attacks or panic disorder, for example, may misread the physical indications associated with fight or flight as signs of impending disaster, and understanding the fight or flight response is thus a useful 'decatastrophizing' strategy.

Similarly, individuals suffering from post-traumatic stress disorder (PTSD) may misinterpret elevated physiological arousal as a sign of an actual threat; learning more about the fight or flight response can help them feel safer and apply relaxation and grounding measures.

Chapter 2

The Positive Aspects of Anger

Anger is a human emotion that can range from slight irritation to uncontrollable anger. In its most basic form, anger indicates that something is wrong with us and that we need to do something about it. When we feel threatened by someone or something, we naturally react with anger. When we are assaulted, it is an empowering sensation that empowers us to fight or defend ourselves. As a result, we require our anger in order to survive. It also helps us establish limits and can be a beneficial force in getting our wants addressed (if we know what our needs are). It is not necessary to be furious in order to have an issue. After all, anger is a normal response that helps us protect ourselves and others. These are several instances where anger can be beneficial and healthy.

Positive effects of anger

It gives us the confidence to defend ourselves or people we care about.

It inspires social action and justice, which encourages us to make the world a better place.

It affirms our uniqueness, especially when we are children.

It serves as a warning to others not to take advantage of us.
It is an extremely effective survival tool.
It is a reaction to pain (physical and psychological).
It is an energy source.
Can encourage you to take action
can inspire you to improve
It may give you power when you feel powerless, helpless, afraid, or victimized.
May function as an alarm clock, alerting you when something is awry.

As compared to good emotions like happiness, enthusiasm, and hope, anger has a bad reputation. Possibly, a lack of respect for anger stems from societal, cultural, and religious factors as well as the obvious manifestations of its frequently disastrous effects, such as hostility and violence. Indeed, many people believe that we would be better off without anger as an emotion. Nonetheless, an increasing number of social and evolutionary psychologists, brain scientists, and mental health specialists believe anger has desirable properties that can benefit the human condition.

From an evolutionary standpoint, all emotions are suitable in particular circumstances when experienced to the greatest extent possible, providing the resources to work efficiently toward a desired goal.

Some amounts of stress and worry, for example, motivate us to perform at a high level. Grief can be cathartic, infusing us with gratitude for what we've lost while indicating to others that we need help recovering and healing. Similarly, mild to moderate anger can help us move forward constructively; nevertheless, intense or persistent anger can be harmful to our well-being.

Anger is more than just an aggressive reaction. It frequently gives us information that allows us to engage with the world around us more effectively (as well as ourselves). If we perceive anger as something that informs us, we can adjust our behavior to improve our position. In light of this, a list of advantages that anger can bring about when it reaches the appropriate level of emotion is provided below.

1. ANGER IS INTENDED TO AID IN SURVIVAL.

Emotions developed to protect us. Anger drives our fight response, which evolved to protect us from an enemy or danger. Anger is rooted in our primal drive to survive and defend ourselves against assault. Anger makes us more aware of potential threats and sharpens our focus. When we are threatened or attacked by a predator, our anger is naturally awakened, prompting us to fight back and act swiftly and powerfully to protect ourselves.

2. CALMING ANGER DISCHARGE

You feel physical and emotional anguish when you are angry. When you are experiencing bodily and emotional discomfort, anger drives you to take action. As a result, anger helps you cope with stress by first discharging the tension in your body and then calming your "nerves," which is why you may have an angry reaction and then feel peaceful.

3. ANGER GIVES YOU A SENSE OF CONTROL.

Anger is linked to a strong desire for control. anger defends what we have, making us feel in command rather than vulnerable. Anger's job is to inflict costs or withhold advantages from others in order to promote our own well-being. People who adequately experience and exhibit their anger have a better chance of meeting their demands and controlling their fate than those who repress their anger. Nonetheless, it is critical to avoid becoming obsessed with the sensation of power that anger might elicit.

4. ANGER FUELS US.

We defend ourselves from a survival standpoint when we retaliate and make others fear us. Anger protects us when someone wishes to harm us. It gives us the strength and ferocity we need to defeat a more powerful foe. Anger serves as a positive force in everyday situations, motivating us to stand up for ourselves and find creative solutions to the challenges we face.

Anger "mobilizes resources, increases vigilance, and facilitates the removal of obstacles in the way of our goal pursuits, particularly if the anger can be divorced from the propensity to harm or destroy."

5. ANGER INSPIRES US TO FIX PROBLEMS

We can become enraged when things seem out of place. If things aren't going as they should and something needs to be done, anger drives us to act and motivates us to solve our problems. Anger is elicited when we encounter an impediment or individual (or anything else) that interferes with our needs. It prepares us to deal with the impediment or obstacle on our way so that we can arrive at our destination.

6. ANGER AWAKENS US TO INJUSTICE

When we are denied our rights or confront insults, contempt, unfairness, or exploitation, we frequently become enraged. Anger acts as an internal cue that things aren't quite right or that someone has treated us unfairly or unjustly. Anger communicates to others, "You'd better treat me honestly; otherwise, you'll pay a hefty price." On a larger scale, standing up to injustice might deter people from taking advantage of others. This form of anger can affect beneficial social change and raise the social penalty for misbehaving.

7. OUR GOALS ARE DRIVEN BY ANGER.

Anger motivates us to achieve our desired goals and rewards. When we do not achieve what we want, we become angry, which signals that we have strayed from our desired goals. Anger seeks to eradicate anything that stands in the way of our desires. It energizes and motivates us to take action in pursuit of our goals and beliefs.

8. ANGER DESTRIES OPTIMISM

Strangely, anger can inspire hope. It might motivate us to focus on what we want to accomplish rather than just the pain, insult, or persecution. The anger system is focused on what is attainable rather than the unreachable. When we are upset, we frequently believe that we have the potential to influence the situation, allowing us to take action and go from an undesirable to a desirable position.

9. ANGER DEFENDS OUR VALUES AND BELIEFS.

Anger functions as a value signal and regulator in social and personal settings. It is triggered when our ideals do not align with the situation we are in. As a result, it makes us conscious of our deep-seated ideas and what we stand for. It also inspires us to correct the mismatch and act to change the situation (or our thinking) in order to align the reality we face with our ideals.

10. ANGER CAN BE USED AS A BARGAINING TOOL.

Anger naturally develops when someone places a lower value, or weight, on your well-being in comparison to their own. Anger is intended to rebalance the situation and raise our worth. Anger also aggressively expresses our position and may lead to others' cooperation. Anger motivates us to respond to conflict in a way that allows us to bargain more effectively. It causes others to reconsider their perspectives in relation to ours. It communicates to the other party, "What you suggest is too expensive for me." You would be better off changing the value you place on me.

11. ANGER BOOSTS COOPERATION

If the anger is warranted and the answer is suitable, the misunderstanding is usually cleared up, resulting in increased collaboration. Anger communicates to others that it is vital to listen to us, that we are annoyed and that it is prudent to pay attention to our comments. Anger expresses itself as "I don't like the situation, and we need to work together to find a better solution." Anger compels you to speak up for yourself and constructively challenge the opposing party. As a result, anger promotes cooperation.

12. ANGER HELPED NEGOTIATE POSITIONS

Anger may produce greater results in business discussions. When two parties are negotiating, the negotiator who appears more agitated may be in a better position to sway the agreement in their favor. Similarly, if one party believes the other party is upset, they may be more prepared to compromise. In this aspect, anger can be utilized as a negotiation strategy to persuade, obtain an agreement, or improve the negotiated position.

13. PAINFUL FEELINGS ARE COVERED BY ANGER

Anger fulfills this vital psychological purpose in the same way that Sigmund Freud's defense mechanisms exist to safeguard the personality from excruciating anxiety when the ego is under attack. anger is a raw, "superficial" emotion that protects you from feeling more difficult feelings. For example, a person who has been betrayed by their partner may use anger to control their partner rather than sharing their own painful anguish.

14. ANGER FORCES US TO GO DEEPER INTO OURSELVES.

Anger is a visceral feeling that can be explosive at times. But, just as a volcano is generated when magma pushes up through the earth's crust from below, depositing lava on the surface, numerous pressures, such as fear and defensiveness, push anger to the surface.

It could be a fear of losing control or of being alone, rejected, abandoned, or unloved, among other things. Anger brings insight into ourselves because it is the most hidden layer of deeper concerns. This is why it is critical to follow the trail of anger and dig deep to identify and address its source. Only once we treat the blockage that causes anger can we be free of the anguish it can cause.

15. ANGER CAN HELP YOU IMPROVE YOURSELF

Anger may transform you into a better person and a force for good. It sheds light on our flaws and failings. When seen positively, this can result in positive effects. Similar to motivation, it has the potential to influence self-improvement. For example, if a person is aware that certain things irritate them, they can work on these triggers to improve their response to them and, as a result, enhance their quality of life and relationships.

16. ANGER IMPROVES EMOTIONAL INTELLIGENCE

People with higher emotional intelligence welcome unpleasant feelings such as anger rather than avoiding or suppressing them. Emotionally intelligent people do not oppose anger but rather use its "knowledge" to obtain its benefits.

As a result, they have more adaptable and resilient emotional response systems and are more adaptable.

Despite its negative connotation, the concept of constructive anger is getting empirical support from researchers and has the potential to improve our lives. anger is a necessary component of our fight-or-flight response. It was formerly a need for survival, and it still has some positive significance now. Anger-fueled motivation and action can propel us forward toward our objectives. It motivates us to remedy the wrongs we perceive in the world.

In life-or-death situations, extreme anger is effective. Yet, this modality is rarely effective in everyday life. The ability to express anger in a manner that is appropriate to the circumstances is essential to its efficacy (rather than repressing it), and using it wisely. According to Aristotle, we must be furious "with the right person, at the right degree, at the right moment, for the right cause, and in the right way."

When we think of anger, we think of its most extreme negative manifestation: anger expressed destructively or inappropriately. Anger is a strong emotion that, when recognized, understood, and channeled correctly, can be highly beneficial.

To begin with, anger simply is; as humans, we will all experience it from time to time. It is damaging to avoid it or pretend it does not exist.

The best way to deal with anger is to feel it and try to figure out where it's coming from. Anger is how we protect ourselves.

It's the big red light in your head that goes out when someone hurts you or crosses a personal boundary. Recognizing your emotions and attempting to comprehend what occurred helps you determine the best course of action, after you calm down, of course.

Problems of suppressing or ignoring Anger

Depression, according to psychologists, is anger channeled inward. In this case, the person may not want to or be terrified of feeling furious, so they turn their anger on themselves. People might say, "I should have known better," for example. That person is unquestionably superior to me; because of this, they were promoted." "I'm having difficulties learning this; I must be out of my mind "He turned me down for another woman. What's the matter with me?" I believe it is always beneficial to examine your contribution to a situation and learn from your experience, but if you are furious with the other person, it is not beneficial.

Fear and worry are another side effect of suppressed anger. We may project what we do not recognize. For example, if I was mocked or abused as a youngster and still have unprocessed anger over it, which is very reasonable, I may be unwilling to trust others.

Instead, I can transfer my anger to others and perceive them as potential bullies. It may have an impact on the quality of my relationships and my capacity to connect with others.

Because anger is such a strong emotion, if it is not addressed, it can manifest itself indirectly and destructively. Individuals frequently use the term passive-aggressive to describe remarks or actions that are indirect and undermining. This dynamic is familiar to all of us. It is the individual who appears to be quite kind on the surface, but their words or actions may have an undercurrent of meanness that reveals their genuine sentiments or intent. You should never be that person.

Channelling Your anger

Anger is a difficult feeling to regulate, but with a little work, you may channel your anger in a more beneficial direction. If you've ever felt compelled to act after becoming furious, you've encountered a beneficial element of this human emotion. Anger can be a tremendous motivator, whether it comes from being wronged, losing a battle, or anything else.

This drive for action following an outburst of anger can be quite beneficial and helpful in assisting you to make changes in your life and determine what is most important to you. Consider anger to be a beneficial piece of information.

But, you may have witnessed the opposite side of the coin and experienced anger's meddling in your life. Perhaps your anger drives you to be overly reactive and to act in ways you later regret.

Learning how to control your anger can be a life-changing skill. When you learn how to harness your anger, you get a great tool.

When you transform your anger into motivation, it can help you self-advocate and create great changes. It motivates self-improvement and encourages leadership in the face of injustice.

Anger has been essential to human survival because it allows people to confront and overcome challenges. Anger is also a speedy adaptive response that shields us from environmental hazards.

Suppressing anger is not advised because it can lead to anxiety and physical problems such as:

Cardiovascular disease

High blood pressure causes heart disorders, which are referred to as heart disease.

Certain heart diseases are caused by the heart functioning under increasing strain. Hypertension in the heart can lead to a variety of conditions, including heart failure, thickened heart muscle, coronary artery disease, and others.

Heart disease can lead to major health issues. It is the major cause of death from hypertension.

Stroke

A stroke happens when a blood vessel in the brain ruptures and bleeds or when the blood supply to the brain is cut off. Blood and oxygen can't arrive at the cerebrum's tissues because of the break or block.

Without oxygen, brain cells and tissue decay and suffocate within minutes.

High blood pressure

Blood pressure is the force that blood exerts on the artery walls as it travels through them. A person's diastolic blood pressure should be less than 120, and their systolic blood pressure should be less than 80.

When the systolic, or upper number, is between 130 and 139 or the diastolic, or lower number, is between 80 and 89, high blood pressure has begun. Blood vessels can be severely damaged if blood pressure remains too high for an extended period of time. Without oxygen, brain cells and tissue die within minutes. This can result in a variety of consequences, some of which can be fatal.

Digestive issues

Digestive disorders are a collection of illnesses that develop when the digestive system does not work properly. Experts divide them into two types: organic and functional gastrointestinal diseases.

Organic GI diseases occur when the digestive system has structural defects that hinder it from functioning normally.

The GI tract seems anatomically normal but does not function properly in functional GI diseases.

Headaches

Headaches are a frequent health issue that almost everyone encounters at some point in their lives.

Things that can cause headaches include:
- Emotional disturbances such as stress, despair, or anxiety
- Medical conditions such as migraines or high blood pressure.
- Physical, as in an injury
- Environmental factors, such as weather

A person's quality of life might be harmed by frequent or severe headaches. Understanding how to identify the type of headache and its origin can aid in taking suitable action.

Skin problems

The symptoms and severity of skin problems such as acne and eczema vary widely. They might be temporary or permanent, and they can also be painful or not. Some are potentially fatal.

Some skin problems are caused by environmental factors, while others may be inherited.

While the majority of skin problems are mild, others may suggest a more significant problem.

Suggestions for channeling your anger

There are methods to channel your anger into a constructive force in your life. Consider the following:

–Evaluate why you're upset.
–Search for ways to improve the situation.
–Recognize your emotional triggers.
–Establish new limits.
–Make use of your anger as a motivator.
–Concentrate only on what is truly important.
–Increase your fitness level

1. EVALUATE WHY YOU'RE UPSET.

Anger does not exist in a vacuum; there is generally an underlying impediment or concern. If you examine what is making you angry, you may be able to pinpoint the cause of the problem rather than directing your anger at the wrong person or situation.

For example, if someone gives you terrible or frustrating news, you may become upset and assume that your anger is directly related to that person.

Yet, if you think about why you're furious, you might realize you're angry at the issue, not the messenger. This may prevent you from raising your voice at someone who is merely attempting to assist you.

2. SEARCH FOR WAYS TO IMPROVE THE SITUATION.

Anger can sometimes be a driving force for change. If your anger is motivated by persistent irritation with your situation, you can channel your anger into action.

This entails first identifying the source of your anger and then considering what aspects of your situation you can improve.

Perhaps it's an unhappy relationship, the urge to leave a horrible living situation, or a poisonous work environment.

Take stock, and then decide what is a reasonable first step toward making a positive change in your life.

3. RECOGNIZE YOUR EMOTIONAL TRIGGERS.

Self-awareness can be extremely beneficial for efficiently controlling and channeling your emotions. If you can pinpoint the source of your anger, you may be able to learn more about your tender spots and emotional triggers. This can help you prepare for the next time you find yourself in a similar situation.

For example, perhaps you react with anger when you believe you are being criticized. Perhaps there is a specific criticism that makes you angry. It can be useful to analyze why that critique is so upsetting.

Journaling when you are angry can help you identify these causes.

When you feel your anger rising, another alternative is to halt and take a few deep breaths. Try to think about the root of your anger for a few moments while you're breathing.

Perhaps you have unsolved insecurities that need to be addressed. Perhaps your partner, parent, or whoever is commenting needs a kind reminder that you don't want to talk about that subject.

A little self-awareness about your emotional triggers might lead to better communication with loved ones or coworkers.

4. ESTABLISH NEW LIMITS.

Personal insight is an important aspect of self-improvement. Anger assists you in discovering your values and priorities. When someone disregards your values, your anger indicates how important those ideals are to you.

Instead of remaining upset, try establishing limits. If you see that someone is consistently ignoring your beliefs and needs, and you are always irritated as a result, it may be time to withdraw yourself from that individual.

5. MAKE USE OF YOUR ANGER AS A MOTIVATOR.

Anger may be extremely motivating. What if someone in your life tells you that you're not capable of landing your ideal job? Let others' skepticism about you fuel your fire.

You understand your worth and ability, and others will soon as well.

6. CONCENTRATE ONLY ON WHAT IS TRULY IMPORTANT

When you are angry, try to pause for a moment and ask yourself, "Will this matter in a year?" Assessing whether something is worth your time and energy is a valuable skill that experience may teach you.

7. INCREASE YOUR FITNESS LEVEL.

Waiting three days for your spin class may not help you manage your anger today. A treadmill in your basement, a flight of stairs, or just a set of hand weights, on the other hand, can help you immediately turn your anger into strength that will improve your fitness.

Anger can be released through exercise. The controlled breathing necessary may help restore a sense of peace. Hence, channeling your anger into fitness can be helpful to both your physical and emotional wellbeing.

How to use Anger as a Motivator

Anger cuts like a knife through the heart. You can feel it, and it hurts, but you're not sure why. Knowing the goal of anger is the best approach to comprehending it.

Even better, if you can affect its intent, you can manage your reactions to it.

Did you realize that anger and motivation have a lot in common?

As an example, motivation is like…

• Anger motivates us to take action.

• When we are upset, we are just concerned with the present.

• In truth, our attention is frequently dominated by a single thing, a single thought.

• Because anger and motivation are inextricably linked, it is easy to be inspired to act on your anger.

Anger frequently results in an aggressive impulse to act. You've undoubtedly witnessed this in yourself. When you are furious with something or someone, you want to disassemble and repair it. It could be a relationship, a situation, or a person, but the need to "fix" it is constant. This provides you with focus and energy.

Motivation operates in a similar manner. When you desire to do something, you are enthusiastic about it. Your heart begins to pound. You're brimming with excitement and energy. Your concentration and energy are also what drive your motivation.

Motivation works best when the desired consequence is small enough. It is more difficult to be motivated to act on your anger when it is significant, such as graduating school or receiving a promotion. You may become agitated and want to make a fuss, but it will not have the same effect. You can be inspired, but not angry. You must utilize both.

Both motivation and anger have their limits. Anger, like motivation, may be a self-defeating force. When you are furious with someone or something, you may say things you later regret. This can make it difficult to get along with that person or scenario. It can also provoke conflict and hostility.

Before you can use anger to motivate yourself, there are a few basic pitfalls to avoid.

Anger is a natural emotion that allows us to express ourselves, release stress, and handle challenging emotions.

When utilized as an incentive, it can, however, become a devastating force. It has the potential to generate a downward spiral and push us further away from our goals.

Anger can make you feel out of control, force you to make rash decisions, lash out and give in to undesirable impulses, and make you give up on your ambitions.

It can exacerbate depression by making you feel helpless and hopeless, and it can cause you to lose confidence. It might also make you feel alienated and lonely.

When anger is not effectively managed, especially when there are deeper issues such as trauma, it may become a self-destructive force that takes control of your life and prevents you from moving forward.

To avoid this, you must maintain a healthy connection with your anger. You must maintain a healthy connection with your anger. Discover how to regulate and convert your anger so that you can be more productive with it.

Preventing your anger from being misdirected

1) Recognize that you must address the source of your anger before you can appropriately channel it.

It's typical to believe that being upset implies we care about something and use anger as a drive. But the truth is that we are easily upset by things that have nothing to do with us. Anger does not always have a justification.

We frequently become enraged because we are upset about something else. Hence, before we get furious, we should try to figure out what has irritated us.

When we are angry, we frequently feel helpless and frustrated because we do not know how to deal with the problem.

We can use anger as a motivator if we first learn to cope with the source of our anger.

This means that we can express our anger without first dealing with the source of it. We may become irritated, aggressive, withdrawn, confused, depressed, furious, or anxious when we are upset about anything. We are feeling so depressed because we don't know how to cope with the root of our anger.

If you see yourself becoming agitated over something you don't understand or can't control, consider what you need to do to cope with it. Occasionally asking for help from a friend or family member can be beneficial, as can taking a break and relaxing.

2) Ask yourself these three questions to get to the bottom of your anger.
a) Where does my anger come from?
b) What is making me so angry? *trigger?*
c) What can I do to address the source of my anger?

If you can't answer the first question, it could mean you need to reconsider your relationship with the person or situation.

For example, if you are furious about your job, it could be because you feel unappreciated or that you are doing all of the work.

The second question concerns the source of your anger. If you can't answer, it suggests the source of your anger isn't evident to you. This could indicate that your anger is being caused by a variety of factors.

The final question concerns what you can do to address the source of your anger. This is the most critical stage in learning how to control your anger. As you get to the root of your anger, you will have a better understanding of what you need to deal with.

The easiest approach to determining whether you should use anger as motivation is to ask yourself:
1. Is my motivation improving my self-esteem?
2. Am I using anger to persuade myself to do something that will help me achieve my objectives?
3. Does my anger cause me to lash out at others?
4. Is my anger interfering with my ability to be positive?

In certain cases, people use their anger to get themselves out of a terrible circumstance. For example, if they are unhappy about the state of their relationship, they may use their anger as an incentive to try to change their relationship with the other person.

Another example would be using anger to accomplish anything. For instance, if you are attempting to clear out your closet and are feeling overwhelmed, it may be beneficial to express your anger in order to drive yourself to complete the task.

This is quite similar to what happens when athletes strive to push themselves to perform one more rep or to cross the finish line. They would frequently yell loudly.

The anger in this scenario is neither directed at oneself nor at others. The anger is simply a burst of focus and energy to aid in the completion of the task.

It makes no difference where the anger comes from. anger can emerge from a variety of sources. For some, the source of their anger is a perceived injustice. Some, on the other hand, use it to feel protected and powerful.

The source of your anger can often influence how you show it. If you become furious at someone else, you may not be able to handle it effectively. If you're upset with yourself, you might try to take it out on someone else. You may feel powerless to resist it if it appears out of nowhere.

But the source of your anger does not have to have power over you. Regardless of the source, anger can be directed positively toward your objectives.

Using anger to effect positive change

Here are a few pointers to help you positivity use your anger:

1) Do not be upset with yourself: Anger is a natural emotion for humans. But sometimes we allow it to spiral out of control and develop into self-hatred.

That is when it turns harmful. Indeed, we need to criticize ourselves from time to time; nevertheless, compassionate self-criticism is more beneficial because it leads to improvement.

2) Have a positive attitude: healthy emotions such as anger and impatience are really strong. When anger is misdirected, though, it may be a terrible force. As a result, it is critical to learn to redirect your anger into something constructive. For example, if you are frustrated with a task or a situation, you can use your frustration to become more efficient and productive. You can also opt to use your anger to assist a friend. In other words, it is always preferable to channel your anger into something positive rather than killing yourself.

3) Understand that anger has a purpose: incorporate both anger and love, thankfulness, and happiness. Remember that we are all humans, and that humans are flawed.
Rather than getting upset at yourself, choose to be appreciative of your achievements. Discover ways to learn from your mistakes and grow as a result of them.

4) Express yourself in writing. anger is not the only emotion that can be expressed in writing. Keeping an emotional diary will help you regulate and understand your emotions. You may feel better in the long term if you write in depth about your anger.
Furthermore, keeping an emotional diary might help you better understand yourself and gain insight.

5) Establish a routine: Many people find it difficult to express their displeasure. But they find other methods to express themselves. They may become agitated at work or yell at a friend. They may also express it in another way.

6) Determine your triggers: It is equally critical to determine your triggers. These are the some of the things that makes you stressed out. It is critical to recognize these things in order to avoid them. This will keep you from being stressed. Remove your triggers if at all possible.

7) Acceptance: If you are having difficulty accepting your anger, attempt to accept it as a normal part of life. You have no or little control over how you feel. Accepting it rather than resisting it is the best option.

8) Self-compassion: Self-compassion is essential. Make an effort to show yourself compassion. When you are experiencing a bad emotion, for example, tell yourself, "I am experiencing sadness, anger, or fear, and I believe that I deserve to feel this way."

9) Meditation: Meditation can help you control your anger and relax your thoughts. Meditation, on the other hand, requires patience. Meditation is a long-term

endeavor. As a result, you must be committed to using it. But the advantages of meditation are well worth the wait. Anger is a very strong emotion, so don't underestimate its strength! It may appear to be a waste of time and energy, yet it can actually propel you to success and pleasure. This is especially true if you use it to motivate and inspire yourself.

Chapter 3

The Negative aspects of anger

Depending on how it is expressed, anger can be a positive or negative feeling. Uncontrolled anger can be extremely harmful to one's mental and physical wellbeing. It can lead to depression, headaches, and other long-term health issues.

Individuals can manage their anger, though, by practicing relaxation techniques, exercising, and seeking counseling. Anger is a strong emotion that can be triggered by annoyance, disappointment, feelings of pain, or impatience. While this emotion can push people to make beneficial changes, suppressing it can have long-term negative effects on the brain and body.

Nobody likes being furious, yet it's a feeling that we all have to deal with. Anger is a natural part of life, and if the body is given time to recuperate, it is not necessarily harmful.

We all understand what it means and how it feels to be angry. But our reactions to anger vary: some people hold it in until they can scribble it down in a journal; others don't even think about it and lash out fiercely instead. This raises the question of whether there is a correct or incorrect method to express anger.

This is a complicated question. Simply put, it is critical that we control our anger effectively in order to avoid negative impacts on our physical or mental health.

Although most people experience anger as a strong dominant emotion, it is frequently regarded as a secondary emotion in psychology. This suggests that whereas the underlying triggering emotions are frustration, abandonment, loneliness, and loss, anger is a straightforward and primitive response.

Anger, as a biological response, releases massive levels of cortisol and adrenaline into the bloodstream, interfering with the body's ability to recover itself in the long run.

Occasional anger is healthy for the body, as long as it is followed by a period of rest to allow the body to cleanse itself of cortisol and adrenaline. Persistent and increasing anger is harmful to the body and is frequently disregarded since a person has grown accustomed to living in a poisonous and overstimulated environment.

It is good and acceptable to be furious from time to time! But if we don't take the time to control and recover from our anger, we risk experiencing unpleasant bodily and mental consequences.

Because of the toll it takes on your body, anger can seriously injure or even kill you. When we are upset, it just takes three seconds for our bodies to enter fight or flight mode, indicating that we are prepared to face an attack.

When we are upset, we stay in this state for about 30 minutes each time we are angry during the day. This causes fatigue and wears on our bodies, resulting in weakened immune systems and an increased risk of illness.

When our bodies are in attack mode, blood pressure and heart rate increase, which can lead to heart attacks or strokes. When dealing with anger issues, many people experience weariness and headaches. While anger is a very necessary feeling to have since it tells us when something is wrong and change is needed, it can be harmful to our health if it occurs frequently and/or lasts for too long."

Anger can fatigue our bodies, resulting in weakened immune systems. A weakened immune system also increases the likelihood of being ill. Therefore, certainly, unresolved or ongoing anger might cause you to become ill more frequently.

If you've ever felt acute, overwhelming anger or witnessed it in another person, you know how it can form in your body. Your heart may be beating, your muscles taut, your hands and jaws clenched, your head throbbing, your nostrils flaring, and your gaze fixed. When these emotions flare up, they have a significant influence on your health.

When you are upset, you become hypervigilant, and your fight-or-flight reaction is activated.

You have a fire in your belly; your face gets red; your blood pressure rises; and you're probably verbalizing this sensation with words or movements, such as throwing your arms up in the air.

Then there's the aftermath, once everything has settled down. You may feel physically exhausted, have sore muscles, have an interrupted mental process, lose concentration, or shed even more tears.

Anger is a terrible emotion! Your body is being thrown off balance by opposing forces, resulting in the reactions you exhibit.

The amygdala, for example, is a portion of your brain that is in charge of emotions and social processing. The prefrontal cortex, on the other hand, is in charge of reasoning and decision-making. Your body attempts to strike a balance between the two. You may not be able to manage your wrath if you do not use your prefrontal cortex.

Stress chemicals such as adrenaline and cortisol are released by your body. In these circumstances, your body goes to war and pays the price. Yet in many circumstances, the price is at least as high (if not higher) for you as it is for the object of your anger.

Effects of Being Angry All the Time on Your Body

Consider the last time you were enraged: the boiling sensation in your gut, your heart hammering, your muscles tightening, and (perhaps) the desire to break whatever was in your path. It turns out that your body is having a moment: all emotions, good, terrible, and everything in between can set off a chain reaction of physical responses that affect everything from your muscular and circulatory systems to your hormones and neurons.

Most of us experience anger on a regular basis. Anger can indicate that you have been wronged in some manner, show potential foes that you are capable of defending yourself, and prepare your body for action in difficult situations.

When you experience anger, your brain assesses if the scenario is potentially harmful to your health. As emotions are processed, they are directed to a structure called the hypothalamus, which is in charge of keeping your body stable and balanced. "What is known as the sympathetic nervous system, or the fight-or-flight response, is initiated by the hypothalamus." Your body in this way delivers chemicals like adrenaline and cortisol, which come about in the physical symptoms described above. Meanwhile, anything that isn't critical to your immediate survival, such as your digestive system, slows down significantly.

It is acceptable to contain anger for a short period of time as long as you eventually deal with your emotions. "There are consistently occurring conditions, in reality, that aggravate you. As long as it passes, it's fine. It's undesirable when it starts to assume control over your life.

A predisposition to hostility, which is used to describe people who are cynical and hostile toward others, might arise from personal fears or difficult situations that make a person feel defensive. You may constantly "put others down and criticize everything."

Frequent complainers may be described as "toxic." "They end up with fewer friends or helpful family members to whom they can turn in times of trouble."

"Your body was not designed to live in that state for long periods of time,". "It's supposed to get you out of a momentary threat." If you let anger overwhelm you, say, and you consistently find yourself angrily ruminating for even a few hours, let alone for days or weeks, a stream of stress hormones will continue to be released into your body, and "this could lead to health problems."

Here's what you should know about the various ways anger can affect your body in the long run, as well as what to do if you're concerned about how it's affecting your health.

1. Increased inflammatory response

Chronic stress, as well as the negative emotions associated with it, are closely connected to greater levels of inflammation in the body and inefficient immune system responses, according to a growing body of research.

Your immune system is designed to use inflammatory cells to tackle possible dangers to your body. "These inflammatory markers also increase when there is persistent stress, such as anger. As a result, if you deal with a lot of anger, even if you don't have an infection, these inflammatory cells may get rowdy and attack healthy cells instead if you deal with a lot of anger. This, in turn, can pave the way for a variety of health difficulties, particularly as you get older.

Furthermore, always feeling anger-y might have an impact on your daily routines, some of which may contribute to additional inflammation or simply harm your health in other ways. " The huge confound we have in any of these studies is that people who are chronically upset tend to participate in lots of bad behaviors," such as smoking, excessive drinking, and bingeing on food that isn't as nutritious as it could be. " Additionally, these bad practices will have an impact."

2. Cardiovascular disease

"We've known for decades that the majority of the research on the health repercussions of anger has to do with the heart and [the rest of the] cardiovascular system."

Try doing a brief body scan the next time your blood starts to boil; that is, take a moment to notice how the various areas of your body feel, one by one, and you'll realize why anger may wreck your heart. "When you continue to ruminate in an angry state, it leads to poor cardiovascular recovery," because "it keeps you in a state of tension."

Anger can raise your blood pressure and heart rate, both of which put enormous strain on your heart muscle and thus increase your risk of chronic hypertension. An influx of stress hormones can also raise your blood sugar and blood fatty acid levels, both of which can damage blood vessels and lead to plaque buildup in the arteries, respectively.

3. Decreased lung function

Many people experience quick and shallow breathing as one of the first physical effects of anger. "It makes sense when we need to "fight or flight" from a dangerous situation,". It's your body's way of trying to supply more oxygen to areas it perceives as essential, such as the brain and muscles. It follows, then, that strong emotions like anger are a common trigger for asthma attacks in those who are susceptible.

However, researchers have discovered that certain emotions may have an impact on your overall lung health.

For example, in one study, 670 older men completed a survey to assess their levels of hostility .

The men also had multiple lung function tests over an eight-year period (lung function naturally declines with age, which can affect how well you breathe;lower score is associated with conditions like asthma and COPD).

The researchers discovered that higher levels of hostility were associated with lower baseline lung function scores as well as a faster rate of lung function decline over time, regardless of whether the men smoked or not. The authors speculate that negative emotions may cause inflammation throughout the body, including the lungs, which can then contribute to the development of various pulmonary diseases.

4. Chronic pain

When you're angry, you may feel heat flowing from your center to areas like your chest, arms, and jaw. "If it's not vented, anger may undoubtedly lead to muscle tightness" Additionally, accumulating a slew of negative feelings can result in significant discomfort or pain.

It's not all in your head. In a study, nearly 500 people with and without migraine were asked to complete questionnaires about their responses to anger; they discovered that those with migraine headaches experienced more intense anger and a lower emotional intelligence score, or the capacity to recognize, comprehend, and control their emotions.

Emotions and neoplastic pain, a term used to describe nonspecific pain that isn't linked to a clear cause like tissue damage, such as the type of pain one might feel from a condition like fibromyalgia, Pain caused by conditions "characterized by ongoing injury," such as osteoarthritis or rheumatoid arthritis, activates parts of the brain involved in regulating emotions.

5. Digestive issues

Your gut, which includes your stomach, large intestine, and small intestine, has its own nervous system; it can function even without your brain and has more neurons than the entire spinal cord, including sensory neurons that monitor what's going on in your gut and motor neurons that control gastrointestinal (GI) contractions that aid in digestion.

When your fight-or-flight response is frequently aroused, the brain can actually alter the contractions involved in digestion, resulting in symptoms such as nausea, constipation, diarrhea, and stomach pain.

It's not surprising, then, that GI disorders like gastroesophageal reflux disease (GERD), irritable bowel syndrome (IBS), and chronic constipation have been linked to a disruption in the gut-brain relationship and that people with GI disorders may be more sensitive to pain signals from the GI tract, which can exacerbate symptoms.

6. Skin rashes

The skin, like the stomach, may react to mental stress. "The improper release of inflammatory chemicals is linked to so many skin diseases." If you already have an inflammatory condition like rosacea, eczema, psoriasis, hormonal acne, or eczema, the inflammation can trigger a flare-up. For example, a 2020 review of 41 studies that looked at the relationship between negative emotions and skin disorders noted that, while little research has specifically looked at anger, some studies seem to link psoriasis and chronic hives to difficulty communicating anger.

Furthermore, how your skin reacts when you're angry is related to how you cope with anger. If you tend to touch or pick at your face a lot when you're stressed, anxious, or irritated, that will only make a breakout worse. Furthermore, if your anger is causing you to miss out on sleep and eat or drink poorly, your skin will suffer as a result.

Although anger can be beneficial at times, it typically has negative implications, including road anger, domestic violence, child abuse, physical assault, and even murder.

The five major costs of anger are as follows:
- The first cost is your health.

Chronic, high levels of anger have been linked to an increased risk of health problems, and how frequently anger is experienced and expressed during times of emotional distress are important elements in determining the influence on one's health.
- The second cost is your self-esteem.

Although expressing anger may feel wonderful in the moment, it frequently leads to emotions of guilt, shame, embarrassment, and remorse. On a cognitive level, one may recognize that his or her response was excessive, misdirected, and/or unnecessary, resulting in self-esteem loss in the majority of situations.
- The third cost is your Relationships

Few things can harm a relationship as much as an inability to control one's anger; frequent and/or intense outbursts, whether verbal or violent, can wreck marriages, tear families apart, and ruin friendships.
- The fourth your Children

Witnessing chronic and/or extreme anger in the home may be damaging for children, often more so than the consequences of parental divorce.
- The fifth cost is the Workplace

Poorly managed anger, irritation, and resentment can seriously undermine what gets done in the workplace, both numerically and qualitatively.

Negative Effects of Anger

Anger is a natural emotion that occurs in response to a dangerous scenario.

Humans created this emotion because they required something to empower them in a hazardous circumstance, something to circumvent their inherent fear and hesitancy and force them into action.

Individuals residing two or a long time ago employed indignation to preserve their house, town, and family against invasions by hostile clans, and it has likewise triggered uprisings, for example, the French Revolution and other independence struggles.

.While anger can be used to motivate positive actions, it is still a negative emotion that can harm your mind and body. In fact, people who experience this emotion on a regular basis are more likely to develop health problems, which are exacerbated by their inability to express their anger, allowing it to fester inside.

Many people used to release their anger through violence, confrontation, and aggression, picking up swords, axes, spears, and hammers to defend their territory, but such reactions are no longer acceptable expressions of this emotion. Instead, we tend to write an angry email or vent on social media.

Anger's Most Harmful Consequences

Anger is a harsh emotion that takes a toll on your body and mind.

People underestimate how damaging it can be and fail to address it. In terms of its effects on your body, it's very similar to stress, and everyone knows how bad that is for you! However, with proper anger management, it is possible to avoid triggers, channel anger productively, and ensure your health isn't affected by it.

Following are some of the most negative consequences of this emotion:

Impact on the mind

When anger is triggered, it bypasses your reasoning ability and causes the body to react, which can make you make rash decisions, act violently, and feel helpless because you can't control things anymore. Most people would rather stay in control and do not want to instinctively express their anger, regardless of whether their emotion is reasonable or unreasonable.

This mental health condition makes people more receptive and prone to unpredictable behavior. Their anger is usually contained within themselves, but it can spill out in different situations. However, people experience depression as a result of anger as well. Their brains become relatively unstable every time they experience anger , which can lead to chemical imbalances or emotional turbulence.

Anxiety: People who are frequently angry are in a heightened state of awareness; they are wary, always on the lookout for threats, and easily triggered, which can lead to anxiety. This mental health concern has a significant impact on a person's life, especially if they develop a proclivity for panic attacks.

Irritability: Anger can build and grow until a relatively calm individual becomes irritable; high levels of irritability lead to frequent outbursts of anger, which eventually make a person more irritable; this cycle must be halted for a person to restore control and tranquility.

Low Self-Esteem: As previously stated, angry people frequently direct their anger inward; their mental voice is negative and attacks a person's self-esteem, which has a significant impact on a person's self-belief, making them reluctant to try new things, experiment with different treatments, or take the initiative.

People who suffer frequent anger typically appear to be confident but aren't; they are sensitive to criticism, reluctant to recognize mistakes, and easily aroused. Anger management, combined with some assertiveness, can help them establish a steadier perspective.

Guilt: Guilt is widespread among people who are prone to expressing their anger aggressively; people frequently take this problem out on their loved ones and friends, which can ruin personal relationships and increase guilt.

Anger has a significant impact on your personal connections, which only worsens the mental state and causes people to fall into profound melancholy. Regrettably, anger and depression frequently go hand in hand.

To regain excellent mental health, both must be handled concurrently. The only way to resolve this issue and get into a better frame of mind is through careful anger management, therapy, positive expression, and increased assertiveness.

Impact on the Body

Anger is a reaction to a threatening circumstance, thus it prepares your body for fight or flight; it is a strong physical response that provides a brief surge of energy and force but fades after the anger has been expended.

This surge can have a significant long-term influence on your body, especially if it occurs frequently and uncontrollably.

Some of the bodily consequences include:

During Anger: When people are angry, their bodies are preparing to fight. They experience a surge of energy as their blood races, their heartbeat speeds up, their breathing becomes more rapid, and their focus narrows.

Their muscles tense in preparation for a fight or retreat. This flood of energy should be ousted emphatically on the grounds that the main sense is consistently savage in its response.

Following Anger: The long-term medical implications of recurrent anger can be serious and even fatal, with people experiencing regular headaches, hypertension, heart difficulties, skin problems, insomnia, and digestive imbalances, as well as an increased risk of strokes or heart attacks.

Angry people are also more likely to get engaged in fights, which can result in injuries and even fatalities; they're more reckless and make judgments that put them in danger, which is why learning to control anger without repressing it is critical.

Your health, self-esteem, relationships, the emotional well-being of your children, and your work productivity can all be negatively impacted by uncontrollable anger. On a larger scale, it may lead to unacceptable behaviors such as road anger, domestic violence, child abuse, assault etc.

Chapter 4

Types of Anger

According to my research, there are two sorts of anger: passive aggression and assertive anger.

Passive Aggression

Passive-aggressive anger is a defensive mode of expression. This form of anger comes when you repress your emotions and try to avoid all types of disputes. Anger can be dangerous since it has a negative impact on your self-esteem. As a result, passive-aggressive anger can be detrimental to your relationships.

Passive-aggressive anger , which can be verbal or physical, is characterized by emotional repression and confrontation avoidance. This might manifest as passive-aggressive remarks (e.g., "I like your clothes, even though they don't fit you"), sarcasm, or a deliberate lack of response. Passive aggressiveness is most commonly shown verbally, but it can also manifest as closed-off body language or constant procrastination at work.

Someone who is passive-aggressive expresses their displeasure in subtle and covert ways.

"Basically, you 'stow away' your little demonstrations of brutality on display, making uninvolved hostility especially deceptive and harming." This includes anything that avoids direct confrontation while still expressing a negative sentiment is considered passive-aggressive behavior. Of course, this provides mixed messages to the person experiencing the hostility, which can be perplexing, frustrating, and lead to emotional distrust. It's also difficult to show that someone is being passive-aggressive, which adds to the confusion.

A person with passive aggression anger will exhibit the following behaviors:

1. Indirect denial

"Refusing to meet someone's demands indirectly is a sort of passive-aggressive behavior." For example, supposing you've asked your spouse or a roommate to do the dishes several times and they haven't explicitly said no, but they don't intend to do the dishes. Certainly, they could be being lazy. Yet they could also be avoiding the dishes on purpose without telling you directly what's going on.

2. Ghosting

Ghosting is a form of passive aggression. Instead of facing the fact that they no longer want to speak with you, a passive-aggressive individual would prefer to leave it all unsaid by never speaking to you again.

3. Arriving late

Passive-aggressive individuals frequently arrive late. This can also appear to be procrastination. The theory is that if a passive-aggressive individual doesn't want to accomplish something, they will put it off until the last minute rather than address their problems directly.

4.Silence

In some situations, silence can be extremely passive-aggressive. This can manifest as
stonewalling in the middle of an argument, ignoring a question, or leaving a text on "read." Silence when a response is required can also be considered passive aggression.

5.Excuses

People will sometimes make up reasons for doing or not doing something rather than expressing their frustrations directly. "Frequently becoming ill in a way that interferes with responsibilities or forgetting crucial meetings or dates" might be considered passive-aggressive.

6.Patronizing

People will sometimes use passive-aggression in their words, such as making patronizing remarks.

Perhaps they insult your knowledge with phrases like "Do you understand what I mean by that?" or again call you titles like "kid" or "honey."

It can be extremely passive-aggressive to do anything that makes them appear to be superior and you to be inferior.

7.Sarcasm

Sarcasm, too, can be passive-aggressive in some situations. For example, if you ask your spouse to a family gathering and they respond in a mocking tone, "Yes, you know how much I love your family," that is passive-aggressive. Rather than honestly discussing their difficulties with your family, they are expressing their negative thoughts by covering them with a joke.

Management Techniques for Passive-Aggressive Individuals

The tips below can assist you in controlling the undesirable actions of your team's passive-aggressive members.

Determine the behavior.

The first step in dealing with passive aggressiveness is to identify it using the tips provided above. This is frequently the most difficult element to discern because it might be subtle.

Deal with passive-aggressive behavior right away to avoid it escalating. Keep notes on circumstances as they occur so you can provide clear instances of what your team member has done so they understand exactly what you're talking about.

Make a Secure Environment
Next, let the person know that it is safe for them to express their problems and troubles to you openly rather than in secret. Make it obvious to them that, as a manager, you do not "shoot messengers" and would prefer that they come to you with their problems rather than burying them.

You must behave in accordance with this. For example, you might encourage, praise, and support people who bring issues to your attention.

Use Language With Caution
Provide accurate comments and use appropriate language. Instead of criticizing that someone is "always" late, bring out the specific times they arrived in the last week or two and offer them an opportunity to explain why. You can then remind them when the workday begins and ask them to arrive on time in the future.

Although it is vital to be direct and confront the matter head-on, avoid using the word "you." This will prevent the other person from feeling attacked and going on the defensive.

Instead, use first-person pronouns like "I," "we," and "our" to convey how their behavior has affected you and your team. For example, instead of saying, "You missed the deadline," you may add, "I observed the report was two days late."

Maintain your cool.
If you react emotionally to your team member, you may aggravate the matter. They may become more isolated and entrenched in their undesirable behaviors if they feel threatened.

Use a measured, even tone of voice when speaking to them. They may not even realize they are being passive-aggressive, so take an empathic approach to alleviate any fear and hostility. But if they continue to act in this manner, and you have already mentioned the matter, you may need to be firmer and consider disciplinary action.

Determine the root cause
If passive-aggressive persons claim to be "fine" despite their conduct, don't take their responses at face value. To get to the bottom of a problem, ask more probing inquiries. Let them explain themselves, but don't let them transfer the blame.

For example, if someone appears to be reacting poorly to a disappointing job decision—perhaps they were passed over for advancement, inquire as to whether their conduct is related to this. Say that you want to understand how they feel and collaborate with them to brainstorm other methods for them to handle the situation more productively. They might, for example, perfect a specific talent so that they have a better chance of promotion the next time.

Give Instruction

Consider using the GROW Model to provide one-on-one coaching to your team member on how to communicate assertively. Engage in role-playing the discussion of particular issues to help participants develop the confidence to do so without being passive or aggressive.

Assertive Anger

Assertive anger is regarded as a constructive mode of expression. Rather than avoiding a dialogue or resorting to yelling or screaming, assertive anger is used as a healthy and useful expression of displeasure to effect positive change.

Assertive anger can manifest as a healthy, safe way of expressing yourself. For example, you could begin a remark with "I feel upset when..." or "I believe..." Assertive anger is linked with acceptable body language and, in some cases, pre-set expectations about how the event will be resolved or processed.

This allows you to express your anger in a way that promotes positive change.

Assertive anger is a form of anger that is expressed directly and effectively. It is frequently used to settle a dispute or attain a purpose.

Assertive anger differs from passive or violent anger, both of which can be destructive to the person expressing it and those around them.

Anger assertiveness can be beneficial since it allows us to communicate our demands and desires in a clear and unambiguous manner. It can also assist us in setting boundaries with others and standing up for ourselves when we are mistreated. But, if not managed appropriately, assertive anger can be devastating. When this occurs, it might result in cruel and/or violent outbursts of wrath.

Assertive Anger Types

There are three ways to exhibit aggressive anger. Each sort of assertiveness presents its own set of difficulties. Let's look at each one individually.

Assertive anger that is calm and controlled

This type of assertive anger is frequently regarded as the healthiest and most efficient method to communicate our irritation or disapproval. When we are furious, we tend to speak louder and employ more assertive body language.

This can be intimidating to others and give them the impression that they are being attacked. It is critical to note that assertiveness does not always imply hostility. We can still be tough and direct without raising our voices or acting threateningly.

Intense or uncontrollable aggressive anger
This type of forceful anger is often seen as less healthy and productive than calm, controlled assertiveness. We may struggle to regulate our emotions and/or our behavior when we are upset. This might result in angry outbursts that are harmful to both ourselves and others. It is critical to remember that assertiveness does not have to imply a loss of control. We may still express our feelings in a courteous and useful manner.

Assertive violence or angry anger
This form of aggressive anger is frequently regarded as the least healthy and effective manner of expressing our annoyance or disapproval. When we are furious, we may turn to violence or hostility to achieve our goals. This can be destructive to ourselves as well as others. It is critical to remember that assertiveness does not always imply aggression. We can remain forceful and straightforward without resorting to physical or verbal violence.

Symptoms and Signs

There are several signs and symptoms that may indicate that we are having difficulty managing our assertive anger in a healthy manner. These are some examples:

• Feeling as if we are always or easily enraged
• Having hurtful or violent outbursts of anger
• Having difficulty controlling our emotions or behavior when we are upset
• Using passive-aggressive language to express our annoyance or discontent
• Participating in hurtful or violent outbursts of anger
• Having difficulty controlling our emotions or behavior when we are upset
• Using passive-aggressive language to express our annoyance or discontent
• Using violence or hostility to obtain what we desire

Strategies for Dealing with Assertive anger

You can handle your aggressive anger in a healthy way by doing the following:

Take some time to relax.
If you are too upset to think clearly, take some time to cool down before acting. This could be taking a walk, counting to ten, or listening to soothing music.

Speak with someone you trust.
Discussing your anger might help you better understand it and figure out how to deal with it in a healthy way. Locate someone you can confide in, such as a friend, family member, or therapist, and tell them what is upsetting you.

Convey your anger forcefully.
After you've calmed down and considered what you want to say, communicate your anger in an assertive manner. This entails being direct, clear, and respectful. Avoid using nasty or aggressive words. It is also critical to listen to the other person's point of view and try to see things from their perspective.

After expressing your anger, follow up.
After expressing your anger, check in with the person with whom you spoke to ensure that they are doing well. This can help repair any harm caused by the disagreement and prevent further conflict.

Determine your triggers.
What are some of your anger-producing activities? Once you've identified your triggers, you can try to avoid them or prepare for them when they occur.

Understanding triggers can also help you recognize when you are becoming upset so you can take action to calm down before it escalates.

Take the time to listen to others.
When someone else is agitated, try to listen to them without passing judgment. This can help to defuse the situation and understand their point of view. Maintaining relationships can also benefit from holding room for someone else's anger.

Get expert assistance.
Get professional help if your anger is producing problems in your life. A therapist can teach you constructive strategies to deal with your anger.

Assertive anger is a sort of anger that can be beneficial in some situations. Nonetheless, it is critical to learn how to express oneself in healthy ways. You may learn how to cope with assertiveness in a constructive and useful way for yourself and those around you by following the guidelines above.

When it comes to assertive anger, it is critical to remember a few fundamental points. Assertiveness does not have to imply hostility or violence, and it is critical to be courteous when expressing your anger. You may learn how to cope with assertiveness in healthy and positive ways if you keep these guidelines in mind.

Other forms of anger include:

Behavioral Anger

Behavioral anger is a physical reaction that is typical among males who struggle with anger. This can be harmful since it might manifest as aggression, perhaps leading to destructive or misplaced anger. Behavioral anger is impulsive and unpredictable, and it might have negative legal or interpersonal implications.

Behavioral anger can take the form of frightening acts such as cornering or raising your voice," "throwing or shoving objects," "smashing objects," or "striking someone," among other things. It is essential to ascertain whether your rage is escalating in this direction due to potential interpersonal or legal repercussions.

Chronic anger

Chronic anger is often aimed at other people, situations, or even yourself, which can have a negative affect on self-esteem. It can sometimes fly under the radar despite causing significant damage.

Chronic anger manifests as a persistent, low-level emotion of anger, resentment, irritation, and annoyance. As previously stated, it can be applied to others, certain situations, or yourself. You may have difficulties processing and expressing your needs as a result of how you experience anger, which can have an influence on your health, stress levels, and relationships.

Destructive Anger

Destructive anger is a severely unhealthy expression of anger that can have a variety of negative consequences. While studies on this sort of anger are sparse, it is frequently associated with the extreme end of behavioral anger. This can involve intense anger or even hatred for others, even when it is unjustified.

Destructive anger can manifest as verbal or physical behaviors that cause harm to others (for example, tossing and shattering something significant to the person you're furious with). In relationships, this might manifest as stonewalling, i.e., shutting out your significant other emotionally. Destructive anger can have a detrimental impact on many aspects of your life, potentially damaging key social bonds.

Judgmental Anger

Judgmental anger is frequently a reaction to a perceived affront, another person's defects, or an injustice against you or someone else. Judgmental anger is recognized in people's core beliefs (a fundamental perspective or knowledge of the world); this core belief is often one of feeling superior or inferior to others, which leads you to criticize and become upset about their actions or expressions. When you or someone else gets upset because of a perceived injustice or affront, this is what is referred to as "justifiable wrath."

This form of anger can also manifest as shaming people or yelling about a perceived injustice. This can harm your interpersonal interactions and hinder your ability to establish a support system. You may also experience feelings of loneliness and low self-esteem.

Overwhelming Anger
Overwhelming anger is unpredictable and can have a negative influence on your mental health over time. This form of anger accumulates, especially when you don't discover ways to express or share your feelings. It may manifest when things reach a "boiling point" or when your ability to cope with anger and stress is overwhelmed as a result of specific situations, feelings, or relationships.

Overwhelming anger can appear as a sudden burst of impatience and hostility after a period of restraint. While everyone's expression of overwhelm differs, it will come on unexpectedly and may be preceded by a stressful experience.

Retaliatory Anger
Retaliatory anger is a common and instinctual reaction to being attacked. It might be inspired by a desire for vengeance following a perceived wrong.

This type of anger is frequently directed at someone who has wronged you. It may be influenced by the desire to acquire control of an event.

After being verbally or physically attacked, you may find yourself directing your anger towards specific people. Retaliatory anger has the capacity to enhance the level of discomfort and hostility in a relationship.

Self-abusive Anger
Shame is often associated with self-abusive wrath. This form of anger is seen in those who have low self-esteem or who feel worthless and hopeless. Self-abusive anger is widely employed to cope with these sentiments, despite the fact that it just drives people away.

Self-abusive anger can have an internal and external impact. Internalizing bad sentiments and acting on them through self-harming behavior, alcohol or drug use, unhealthy and disordered food, or negative self-talk (e.g., "You are a failure."). On the surface, this can appear as lashing out or verbally attacking others.

Silent Anger
Quiet anger is a nonverbal, internal expression of anger. Others may be able to read your anger even if you do not express it verbally. Silent anger causes people to keep their sentiments inside and allow them to build up, which can lead to greater stress, tension, and behaviors associated with overwhelmed anger.

Quiet anger can be either internal or outward. Internally, this form of anger can lead to an accumulation of unspoken irritation, anger, and resentment, generating unnecessary stress and low levels of continuing tension. It might appear externally as closed-off body language and facial expressions, as well as restricted or minimal speech and tone.

Verbally Spoken Anger
Verbal anger is an aggressive form of anger that can turn abusive. Individuals who experience this form of anger have been seen to feel terrible after striking out at the object of their anger and may even apologize after an episode.

Lashing out or "going off" on someone verbally might be signs of verbal anger . Loud shouting, threatening behavior, scathing comments, constant and harsh criticism, and ridiculing are examples of specific behaviors. Bear in mind that verbal anger can quickly escalate into verbal abuse. It can also make it difficult to sustain stable or healthy relationships.

Volatile Anger
Volatile anger, often known as "sudden anger ," is an explosive sort of anger that can occur when someone perceives an annoyance, major or minor, and explodes verbally or physically, potentially becoming dangerous. This form of anger makes it difficult for the person to express, process, and communicate.

Volatile anger might appear as a fast shift from the status quo to wrath over real or perceived slights.

It is typically destructive, involving shouting, yelling, throwing objects, and physical aggression. This form of anger may make it difficult for you to build secure and trustworthy relationships.

Chapter 5

Anger Management

Anger can be expressed in a variety of ways, and the causes of anger can also vary. Identifying the source and nature of your anger is an important first step toward learning to regulate and manage it.

We all understand what anger is and have experienced it, whether as a passing annoyance or full-fledged anger. anger is a fully normal and, in most cases, healthy human emotion. Nevertheless, when it becomes destructive and out of control, it can cause problems at work, in personal relationships, and in the general quality of your life.

Anger can make you feel like you're at the mercy of a volatile and powerful feeling. It can be triggered by both external and internal occurrences. You may be furious at a specific person or incident , or you may be upset as a result of worrying or brooding about personal concerns. Anger can be triggered by memories of painful or upsetting situations.

Responding violently is the instinctual, natural way to express anger. Anger is a natural, adaptive response to danger; it enables us to fight and defend ourselves when we are assaulted by motivating intense, frequently aggressive sentiments and behaviors. As a result, a certain level of anger is required for human survival.

On the other hand, we can't physically lash out at every person or object that upsets or annoys us; laws, societal conventions, and common sense limit how far our anger can go.

Individuals deal with their furious sentiments through a number of conscious and unconscious mechanisms. There are three approaches: expressing, concealing, and calming. The healthiest approach to communicating anger is in an authoritative, rather than aggressive, manner. To accomplish this, you will need to acquire the skills necessary to effectively communicate your demands and negotiate their fulfillment without causing harm to other people. Being assertive does not necessitate being coercive or insistent; rather, it implies respect for oneself and others.

Anger can be controlled before it can be turned or redirected. This occurs when you suppress your anger, stop thinking about it, and concentrate on something constructive. The goal is to control or restrain your anger and redirect it into more beneficial action. The problem with this type of reaction is that if it is not allowed to show itself outwardly, your wrath can shift inward—on yourself. Depression, high blood pressure, and hypertension are all possible outcomes of internalized anger.

Anger that is not voiced might lead to other issues. It can result in pathological forms of anger, such as passive-aggressive behavior, or a personality that appears eternally cynical and angry.

Those individuals who are constantly shaming others, praising everything, and making cynical remarks have not learned how to constructively express their anger. They are probably not going to have numerous effective organizations, which isn't unforeseen.

Anger management techniques

Relaxation

Basic relaxation techniques, such as deep breathing and relaxing imagery, can aid in the reduction of furious sensations. There are books and classes that can teach you relaxation techniques, which you can use in any situation once you learn them. If you're in a relationship with a hot-tempered partner, it could be a good idea for both of you to master these strategies.

These are some basic steps you can take:
Relaxation comes from deep diaphragmatic breathing. Not if you breathe through your chest. Gently repeat a calm word or phrase such as "relax breathing from your chest will not. Gently repeat a calm word or phrase such as "relax" or "take it easy" to yourself while breathing deeply.". Use imagery; envision a soothing moment, from either your memory or your imagination.

Nonstrenuous, gradual yoga-like activities will relax your muscles and make you feel much calmer.

Use these tactics on a daily basis. Learn to employ them automatically in stressful situations.

Cognitive reorganization

Simply defined, this entails altering your way of thinking. Anger causes people to curse, swear, or use very colorful language that reflects their inner feelings. When you're furious, your thoughts can become exaggerated and theatrical. Substitute more rational thoughts for these irrational ones. Rather than telling yourself, "Goodness, it's awful, it's terrible, everything's wrecked," remind yourself, "It's irritating, and it's understandable that I'm unhappy about it, but it's not the end of the world, and being angry won't cure anything either."

When talking about yourself or someone else, avoid using phrases like "never" or "always." "This machine never works" or "you're always "neglecting stuff",they always give you the impression that your anger is justified and that there is no remedy to the issue. They also alienate and degrade people who would otherwise collaborate with you to find a solution. Remind yourself that being angry will not solve anything and will not make you feel better. Logic triumphs over anger because, even when justified, anger can soon become unreasonable. So apply cold, hard reasoning to yourself.

Tell yourself that the world isn't trying to get you; you're just going through the motions of daily existence. Do this every time you feel your anger getting the best of you, and you'll gain a more balanced viewpoint. Anger makes individuals expect things like fairness, gratitude, agreement, and the readiness to do things their way. Everyone wants these things, and we're all disappointed and wounded when we don't get them, but furious individuals demand them, and when their expectations aren't granted, their disappointment turns to anger.

As part of their cognitive restructuring, adolescents must become conscious of their demanding tendencies and transform their expectations into wishes. In other words, saying "I would like" something is preferable to saying "I demand" or "I must have." When you are unable to obtain what you desire, you will experience the expected feelings of frustration, disappointment, and hurt—but not wrath. Some furious people use their anger to avoid feeling wounded, but this does not mean the hurt is gone.

Resolving issues

Sometimes our anger and irritation are the result of very genuine and unavoidable challenges in our lives. Not all anger is misdirected, and it's often a healthy, natural reaction to these challenges. There is also a cultural belief that every problem has a solution, which adds to our disappointment when we discover that this isn't always the case.

The ideal attitude to bring to such a scenario is to focus on how you handle and face the problem rather than on finding a solution.

Create a plan and track your progress as you go. Commit to giving it your all, but don't punish yourself if you don't get an answer immediately . Even if the problem does not get solved right away, if you approach it with the greatest intentions and efforts and make a sincere attempt to meet it head-on, you will be less likely to lose patience and slip into all-or-nothing thinking.

Improved communication

Angry people have a tendency to jump to and act on conclusions, which can be quite wrong. The first thing you should do is slow down and think through your comments if you're in a heated debate. Slow down and think carefully about what you want to say, rather than saying the first thing that comes to mind. Simultaneously, give the other person your full attention and take your time before responding.

Pay attention to what is causing the anger. For instance, you value your personal space and degree of independence more than your "significant other" does. If he or she begins to complain about your activities, do not counterattack by portraying your partner as a jailer, warden, or albatross around your neck.

When you are chastised, it is natural to become defensive, but do not fight back. Instead, pay attention to what's beneath the words: the message that this person may feel neglected and unwanted. It may take some patient probing on your part, as well as some breathing space, but don't allow your anger or that of your partner to spin out of control. Maintaining your cool can help you avoid a bad situation.

Making use of humor

In a variety of ways, "silly humor" might defuse anger. For one thing, it can assist you in gaining a more balanced perspective. When you're upset and call someone a name or use an imaginative phrase to refer to them, take a moment to imagine what that word might actually look like. If you imagine a coworker as a "dirtbag" or a "single-cell life form" at work, imagine a giant bag full of dirt (or an amoeba) sitting at your colleague's desk, talking on the phone, and attending meetings. Do this whenever a name concerning another person comes to mind. If you can, provide an image of what the actual object could look like. This will take a lot of the sting out of your anger, and humor can always be counted on to help untangle a knotty problem.
The underlying message of very agitated people is "things should go my way!"

"Angry people often believe that they are ethically correct, that any obstruction or change in their plans is an agonizing humiliation, and that they should not have to suffer in this manner; others might, but not them!

When you have that impulse, consider yourself as a deity or goddess, a great monarch who owns the streets, stores, and office space, walking alone and having your way in all situations while others kowtow to you. The more detail you can put into your imagined scenes, the more likely it is that you are being unreasonable; you will also understand how insignificant the things you are furious about are. There are two things to keep in mind when using humor. First, instead of simply "laughing off" your difficulties, utilize humor to help you tackle them more productively. Second, avoid harsh, sarcastic humor; it's just another harmful type of anger expression.

These strategies all share a reluctance to take yourself too seriously. Although anger is a severe feeling, it is frequently accompanied by ideas that, when analyzed, can make you chuckle.

Adjusting your surroundings

Sometimes it's our immediate circumstances that irritate and enrage us. Issues and duties can weigh on you and make you upset at the "trap" you appear to have fallen into, as well as all the people and things that comprise that trap.

Let yourself a rest. Plan some "personal time" for days when you know it will be especially stressful.

Discuss your emotions.

Talking out an issue or expressing your concerns to someone who has a calming influence on you may be beneficial. But it's crucial to remember that venting can backfire.

Complaining about your boss, explaining all of the reasons you dislike someone, or whining about all of your perceived injustices may fuel the fire. One prevalent myth is that you must express your anger in order to feel better.

Similarly, if you're going to talk to a friend, make sure you're working on a solution or lessening your anger rather than just ranting. It's unjust to utilize them as a sounding board. Alternatively, you may discover that the ideal approach to employing this strategy is to talk about something other than the issue that is making you furious.

Recognizing Your Alert Signs

If you're like some people, you may feel like your anger comes out of nowhere. Perhaps you can switch from calm to furious in an instant. But there are still warning signals that your anger is on the rise. Identifying them early on will help you take measures to keep your anger from boiling over.

Consider the physical symptoms of anger that you experience. Your face may be hot, or your heart may be racing. Or perhaps you start clenching your fists. You might also notice some cognitive alterations. Sometimes your thoughts start racing or you start "seeing red."

By identifying your warning signs, you may take fast action and avoid doing things that can cause worse difficulties. Pay attention to how you're feeling, and you'll improve your ability to see warning signs.

Remove yourself from the triggering situation.

Attempting to win an argument or staying in a bad circumstance will just feed your anger. If possible, remove yourself from the situation as one of the finest anger control exercises.

If you frequently get into intense arguments with someone, such as a friend or family member, talk to them about the necessity of taking a break and restarting when you're both feeling calm.

When you need to take a break, explain that you're not attempting to avoid unpleasant topics but that you're working on anger management. When you're upset, it's difficult to have a fruitful talk or resolve a disagreement. When you're feeling more relaxed, you can resume the discussion or address the matter again.

Setting a precise time and place to discuss the topic again can be beneficial.

This gives your friend, colleague, or family member peace of mind that the matter will be addressed—just at a later date.

More suggestions for loosening up on yourself:
Timing: If you and your spouse tend to argue when you discuss critical issues at night—perhaps because you're sleepy or distracted, or It's simply propensity, take a stab at changing the times when you examine fundamental issues to stay away from conflicts.

Avoidance: If walking by your child's chaotic room gets you angry, close the door. Avoid forcing yourself to examine the things that irritate you. Avoid saying things like, "Well, my child should wash all the dishes so I don't have to be angry!" " That isn't the point. The goal is to maintain your cool.

Seeking alternatives: If your regular commute through traffic makes you angry and frustrated, make it a quest to discover or sketch out a new route that is less congested or more scenic. Alternatively, think about taking a commuter train or bus.

Laughter: Nothing can turn a poor mood around like a good one. Dispel your anger by finding ways to laugh, whether it's by playing with your children, watching stand-up comedy, or scrolling through memes.

Empathy: Strive to put yourself in the shoes of the other person and experience the issue through their eyes. You may obtain a fresh insight and become less furious if you narrate the narrative or recreate the events as they perceived them.

Importance of anger management exercises

Most of us have "lost it" during a heated family feud or while caught in traffic on our way to work. While anger is unpleasant, it can inspire us to alter things that aren't working for us, such as marital problems or difficult work situations.

Yet anger is a powerful emotion. If left uncontrolled, it can lead to depression or other mental health issues. It can also make you act irrationally or angrily. This can lead to social isolation, health issues, and abuse.

Anger is more common among some people than among others. Individuals who are under a lot of stress may have difficulty regulating their anger. Researchers discovered that toddlers with mental health problems and individuals with traumatic brain injuries are more likely to experience intense anger.

There is assistance and support available. In each of these at-risk groups, anger management exercises enhanced well-being and reduced the number of furious outbursts.

If you have trouble controlling your anger, these exercises may be beneficial to you as well.

Anger outbursts can be harmful to you and those around you.

Anger management exercises are a fantastic method to cool down and avoid harm. These approaches operate by first calming you down and then assisting you in making positive progress.

Practice the following anger management exercises until you feel calm whenever you feel your anger is overwhelming:

Learn to breathe properly.

When you're furious, your breathing may become faster and shallower. Slowing and deepening your breathing is an easy way to relax your body and minimize your anger.

Inhale slowly through your nose and exhale slowly through your mouth. Take a deep breath from your abdomen rather than your chest. Breathe in and out as needed.

Progressive Muscle relaxation

Another indicator of stress in the body that you may experience when you are furious is muscle tension.

You could attempt a progressive muscle relaxation technique to help you relax. Each muscle group in the body is carefully tensed and then relaxed one at a time.

Start from the top of your head and work your way down to your toes, or vice versa.

Imagine yourself being at ease

Visualizing a calm location may assist you in reducing your anger. Close your eyes for a few moments and sit in a peaceful, pleasant place in your memory. Allow your imagination to run wild.

Consider little elements as you imagine that calm location. What does it smell or sound like? Consider how peaceful and good you feel in that location.

Get going!

Regular exercise is incredibly efficient at lowering stress in the body and mind, in addition to being healthy for your biological processes. To keep stress and anger at bay, try to get some exercise every day.

A fast walk, bike ride, or run can help you manage your anger quickly. As you feel your wrath rising, engage in some physical activity.

Identify your personal triggers

People usually become enraged over the same things over and over. Spend some time considering what makes you furious. If at all feasible, try to avoid or cope with those things.

For example, instead of getting furious over the clutter, you may close the door to your child's room when they don't clean it.

Using public transit rather than driving to work could be an alternative for you if you're easily bothered by traffic.

Take a moment to listen

When you're in a heated disagreement, you may find yourself leaping to conclusions and saying hurtful things. Making an effort to pause and listen to the other person in the conversation before reacting will help your anger subside, allowing you to reply and settle the situation more effectively.

Before responding, give it some thought. Inform them you need to take a step back if you need to cool off before continuing the talk.

Modify your perspective.

Anger might make you believe that things are worse than they are. Replace negative thoughts with more realistic ones to reduce your anger. When considering this, avoid using extreme phrases such as "never" or "always."

Some effective tactics include maintaining a balanced perspective on the world and changing your angry demands into pleas instead.

Avoid focusing on the same issues repeatedly

Even if the matter has been resolved, you may revisit the same circumstance that offended you. This is referred to as dwelling or ruminating. Dwelling encourages anger to fester, potentially leading to further arguments or other problems.

Strive to move past the source of your anger. Instead, attempt to focus on the positive aspects of the person or scenario that hurt you.

Understand your body
When you are upset, your body becomes tremendously stimulated. Your heart rate, blood pressure, respiratory rate, and body temperature may all rise. Your body also produces stress hormones, which put your body on high alert.

When you're upset, pay attention to your body. Discover your body's warning indications of anger. When you experience these warning signs, take a step back or try a relaxing method.

If your anger has been causing difficulties in your life and you're unable to control it on your own, you should seek professional treatment. Anger control issues can be linked to some mental health concerns.

PTSD, for example, has been linked to aggressive behavior. Depressive illnesses can also increase irritability and make it more difficult to control one's temper.

It is critical to identify any mental health concerns that may be impeding your capacity to manage your anger.

Begin by discussing your mood and behavior with a doctor. A doctor will check to see if you have any physical health conditions that are contributing to the problem.

A doctor may recommend you to a mental health specialist for additional assessment. You may attend anger management therapy, depending on your goals and treatment needs, during which you will learn additional anger management therapy strategies and how to integrate them into your daily life—especially when you are feeling triggered.

Conclusion

Many people regard wrath as something terrible, bad, and problematic, although anger is not necessarily detrimental. Anger becomes bothersome when it is transmitted in improper or destructive ways. Yet, there are various things that can be done to support the effective use of angry emotions.

And don't forget The first step in managing anger is being aware of it. Learn how anger affects you, how you manage it, and what generates it in you. There are numerous techniques to handle anger, as covered in the book, if you learn to detect it and catch it early on.

Printed in Great Britain
by Amazon